Multiplication and Division

Arrays and Shares

Grade 4
Also appropriate for Grade 5

Karen Economopoulos
Cornelia Tierney
Susan Jo Russell

Developed at TERC, Cambridge, Massachusetts

Dale Seymour Publications®

The *Investigations* curriculum was developed at TERC (formerly Technical Education Research Centers) in collaboration with Kent State University and the State University of New York at Buffalo. The work was supported in part by National Science Foundation Grant No. MDR-9050210. TERC is a nonprofit company working to improve mathematics and science education. TERC is located at 2067 Massachusetts Avenue, Cambridge, MA 02140.

This project was supported, in part,
by the
National Science Foundation
Opinions expressed are those of the authors
and not necessarily those of the Foundation

This book is published by Dale Seymour Publications®, an imprint of the Alternative Publishing Group of Addison-Wesley Publishing Company.

Project Editor: Priscilla Cox Samii
Series Editor: Beverly Cory
Manuscript Editor: Ann Marie Brennan
ESL Consultant: Nancy Sokol Green
Production/Manufacturing Director: Janet Yearian
Production/Manufacturing Coordinator: Barbara Atmore
Design Manager: Jeff Kelly
Design: Don Taka
Illustrations: Margaret Sanfilippo, Hollis Burkhart
Cover: Bay Graphics

DALE
SEYMOUR
PUBLICATIONS®
P.O. BOX 10888
PALO ALTO, CA 94303

Order number DS21248
ISBN 0-86651-810-X
4 5 6 7 8 9 10-ML-00 99 98 97 96

T E R C

Principal Investigator   Susan Jo Russell

Co-Principal Investigator   Cornelia C. Tierney

Director of Research and Evaluation   Jan Mokros

Curriculum Development

Joan Akers
Michael T. Battista
Mary Berle-Carman
Douglas H. Clements
Karen Economopoulos
Ricardo Nemirovsky
Andee Rubin
Susan Jo Russell
Cornelia C. Tierney
Amy Shulman Weinberg

Evaluation and Assessment

Mary Berle-Carman
Abouali Farmanfarmaian
Jan Mokros
Mark Ogonowski
Amy Shulman Weinberg
Tracey Wright
Lisa Yaffee

Teacher Development and Support

Rebecca B. Corwin
Karen Economopoulos
Tracey Wright
Lisa Yaffee

Technology Development

Michael T. Battista
Douglas H. Clements
Julie Sarama Meredith
Andee Rubin

Video Production

David A. Smith

Administration and Production

Amy Catlin
Amy Taber

Cooperating Classrooms for This Unit

Kay O'Connell
Linda Verity
Arlington Public Schools, Arlington, MA

Angela Philactos
Michele DeSilva
Jim Samson
Boston Public Schools, Boston, MA

Consultants and Advisors

Elizabeth Badger
Deborah Lowenberg Ball
Marilyn Burns
Ann Grady
Joanne M. Gurry
James J. Kaput
Steven Leinwand
Mary M. Lindquist
David S. Moore
John Olive
Leslie P. Steffe
Peter Sullivan
Grayson Wheatley
Virginia Woolley
Anne Zarinnia

Graduate Assistants

Kent State University:
Joanne Caniglia, Pam DeLong, Carol King

State University of New York at Buffalo:
Rosa Gonzalez, Sue McMillen,
Julie Sarama Meredith, Sudha Swaminathan

CONTENTS

Investigations in Number, Data, and Space is a K–5 mathematics curriculum with four major goals:

- to offer students meaningful mathematical problems
- to emphasize depth in mathematical thinking rather than superficial exposure to a series of fragmented topics
- to communicate mathematics content and pedagogy to teachers
- to expand substantially the pool of mathematically literate students

The *Investigations* curriculum embodies an approach radically different from the traditional textbook-based curriculum. At each grade level, it consists of a set of separate units, each offering 2–4 weeks of work. These units of study are presented through investigations that involve students in the exploration of major mathematical ideas.

Approaching the mathematics content through investigations helps students develop flexibility and confidence in approaching problems, fluency in using mathematical skills and tools to solve problems, and proficiency in evaluating their solutions. Students also build a repertoire of ways to communicate about their mathematical thinking while their enjoyment and appreciation of mathematics grow.

The investigations are carefully designed to invite all students into mathematics—girls and boys; diverse cultural, ethnic, and language groups; and students with different strengths and interests. Problem contexts often call on students to share experiences from their families, cultures, and communities. The curriculum eliminates barriers— such as work in isolation from peers or emphasis on speed and memorization—that exclude some students from participating successfully in mathematics. The following aspects of the curriculum ensure that all students are included in significant mathematics learning:

- Students spend time exploring problems in depth.
- They find more than one solution to many of the problems they work on.
- They invent their own strategies and approaches rather than relying on memorized procedures.
- They choose from a variety of concrete materials and appropriate technology, including calculators, as a natural part of their everyday mathematical work.
- They express their mathematical thinking through drawing, writing, and talking.
- They work in a variety of groupings—as a whole class, individually, in pairs, and in small groups.
- They move around the classroom as they explore the mathematics in their environment and talk with their peers.

While reading and other language activities are typically given a great deal of time and emphasis in elementary classrooms, mathematics often does not get the time it needs. If students are to experience mathematics in depth, they must have enough time to become engaged in real mathematical problems. We believe that a minimum of five hours of mathematics classroom time a week—about an hour a day—is critical at the elementary level. The plan and pacing of the *Investigations* curriculum are based on that belief.

For further information about the pedagogy and principles that underlie these investigations, see the Teacher Notes throughout the units and the following books:

- *Implementing the* Investigations in Number, Data, and Space™ *Curriculum*
- *Beyond Arithmetic*

The *Investigations* curriculum is presented through a series of teacher books, one for each unit of study. These books not only provide a complete mathematics curriculum for your students but also offer materials to support your own professional development. You, the teacher, are the person who will make this curriculum come alive in the classroom; the book for each unit is your main support system.

While reproducible resources for students are provided, the curriculum does not include student books. Students work actively with objects and experiences in their own environment and with a variety of manipulative materials and technology, rather than with workbooks and worksheets filled with problems. We also make extensive use of the overhead projector as a way to present problems, to focus group discussion, and to help students share ideas and strategies. If an overhead projector is available, we urge you to try it as suggested in the investigations.

Ultimately, every teacher will use these investigations in ways that make sense for his or her partic-

ular style, the particular group of students, and the constraints and supports of a particular school environment. We have tried to provide with each unit the best information and guidance for a wide variety of situations, drawn from our collaborations with many teachers and students over many years. Our goal in this book is to help you, as a professional educator, implement this mathematics curriculum in a way that will give all your students access to mathematical power.

Investigation Format

The opening two pages of each investigation help you get ready for the student work that follows. Here you will read:

What Happens—a synopsis of each session or block of sessions.

Mathematical Emphasis—the most important ideas and processes students will encounter in this investigation.

What to Plan Ahead of Time—materials to gather, student sheets to duplicate, transparencies to make, and anything else you need to do before starting.

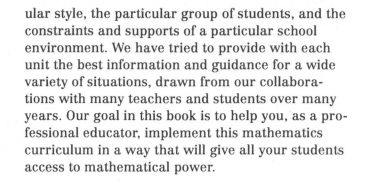

Sessions Within an investigation, the activities are organized by class session, a session being a one-hour math class. Sessions are numbered consecutively through an investigation. Often several sessions are grouped together, presenting a block of activities with a single major focus.

When you find a block of sessions presented together—for example, Sessions 1, 2, and 3—read through the entire block first to understand the overall flow and sequence of the activities. Make some preliminary decisions about how you will divide the activities into three sessions for your class, based on what you know about your students. You may need to modify your initial plans as you progress through the activities, and you may want to make notes in the margins of the pages as reminders for the next time you use the unit.

Be sure to read the Session Follow-up section at the end of the session block to see what homework assignments and extensions are suggested as you make your initial plans.

While you may be used to a curriculum that tells you exactly what each class session should cover, we have found that the teacher is in a better position to make these decisions. Each unit is flexible, and may be handled somewhat differently by every teacher. While we provide guidance for how many sessions a particular group of activities is likely to need, we want you to be active in determining an appropriate pace and the best transition points for your class.

Ten-Minute Math At the beginning of some sessions, you will find Ten-Minute Math activities. These are designed to be used in tandem with the investigations, but not during the math hour. Rather, we hope you will do them whenever you have a spare 10 minutes—maybe before lunch or recess or at the end of the day.

Ten-Minute Math offers practice in key concepts, but not always those being covered in the unit. For example, in a unit on using data, Ten-Minute Math might revisit geometric activities done earlier in the year. Complete directions for the suggested activities are included at the end of each unit. A compilation of Ten-Minute Math activities is also available as a separate book.

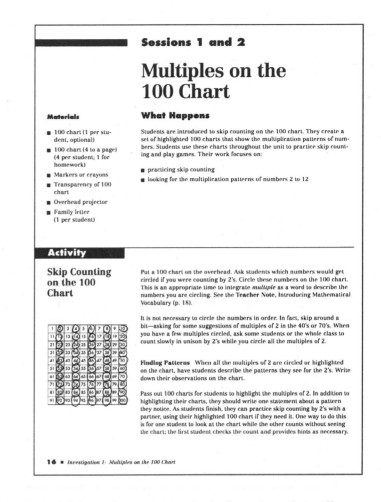

Activities The activities include pair and small-group work, individual tasks, and whole-class discussions. We assume students are seated together, talking and sharing ideas during all work times. Students most often work cooperatively, although each student may record work individually.

Choice Time In some units, some sessions are structured with activity choices. In these cases, students may work simultaneously on different activities focused on the same mathematical ideas. Students choose which activities they want to do, and they cycle through them.

You will need to decide how to set up and introduce these activities and how to let students make their choices. Some teachers present them as station activities, in different parts of the room. Some list the choices on the board as reminders or have students keep their own lists.

Tips for the Linguistically Diverse Classroom
At strategic points in each unit, you will find concrete suggestions for simple modifications of the teaching strategies to encourage the participation of all students. Many of these tips offer alternative ways to elicit critical thinking from students at varying levels of English proficiency, as well as from other students who find it difficult to verbalize their thinking.

The tips are supported by suggestions for specific vocabulary work to help ensure that all students can participate fully in the investigations. The Preview for the Linguistically Diverse Classroom (p. 12) lists important words that are assumed as part of the working vocabulary of the unit. Second-language learners will need to become familiar with these words in order to understand the problems and activities they will be doing. These terms can be incorporated into students' second-language work before or during the unit. Activities that can be used to present the words and make them comprehensible are found in the appendix, Vocabulary Support for Second-Language Learners (p. 76).

In addition, ideas for making connections to students' language and cultures, included on the Preview page, help the class explore the unit's concepts from a multicultural perspective.

Session Follow-Up

Homework Homework is not given daily for its own sake but periodically as it makes sense to have follow-up work at home. Homework may be used for (1) review and practice of work done in class; (2) preparation for activities coming up in class—for example, collecting data for a class project; or (3) involving and informing family members.

Some units in the *Investigations* curriculum have more homework than others, simply because it makes sense for the mathematics that's going on. Other units rely on manipulatives that most students won't have at home, making homework difficult. In any case, homework should always be directly connected to the investigations in the unit or to work in previous units—never sheets of problems just to keep students busy.

Extensions These follow-up activities are opportunities for some or all students to explore a topic in greater depth or in a different context. They are not designed for "fast" students; mathematics is a multifaceted discipline, and different students will want to go further in different investigations. Look for and encourage the sparks of interest and enthusiasm you see in your students and use the extensions to help them pursue these interests.

Family Letter A letter you can send home to students' families is included with the blackline masters for each unit. We want families to be informed about the mathematics work in your classroom; they should be encouraged to participate in and support their children's work. A reminder to send home the letter appears in one of the early investigations. (These letters are also available separately in the following languages: Spanish, Vietnamese, Cantonese, Hmong, and Cambodian.)

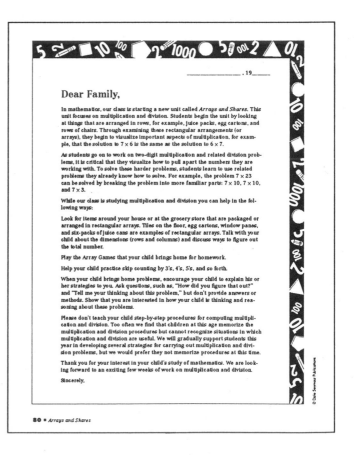

Materials

A complete list of the materials needed for the unit is found on p. 10. Some of these materials are available in a kit for the *Investigations* grade 4 curriculum. Individual items can also be purchased as needed from school supply stores and dealers.

In an active mathematics classroom, certain basic materials should be available at all times: interlocking cubes, pencils, unlined paper, graph paper, calculators, things to count with, and measuring tools. Some activities in this curriculum require scissors and glue sticks or tape. Stick-on notes and large paper are also useful materials throughout.

So that students can independently get what they need at any time, they should know where these materials are kept, how they are stored, and how they are to be returned to the storage area. For example, interlocking cubes are best stored in towers of ten; then, whatever the activity, they should be returned to storage in groups of ten at the end of the hour. You'll find that establishing such routines at the beginning of the year is well worth the time and effort.

Student Sheets and Teaching Resources

Reproducible pages to help you teach the unit are found at the end of this book. These include masters for making overhead transparencies and other teaching tools, as well as student recording sheets.

Many of the field-test teachers requested more sheets to help students record their work, and we have tried to be responsive to this need. At the same time, we think it's important that students find their own ways of organizing and recording their work. They need to learn how to explain their thinking with both drawings and written words, and how to organize their results so someone else can understand them.

To ensure that students get a chance to learn how to represent and organize their own work, we deliberately do not provide student sheets for every activity. We recommend that your students keep a mathematics notebook or folder so that their work, whether on reproducible sheets or their own paper, is always available to them for reference.

Name _____ **Date** _____

Student Sheet 1

Multiplication Clusters

Solve each cluster of multiplication problems. Look for ways the problems in each cluster are related.

$2 \times 4 =$ $4 \times 4 =$ $\begin{array}{r} 8 \\ \times 4 \end{array}$ $\begin{array}{r} 12 \\ \times 4 \end{array}$

$7 \times 2 =$ $\begin{array}{r} 8 \\ \times 2 \end{array}$ $9 \times 2 =$

$5 \times 6 =$ $6 \times 6 =$ $\begin{array}{r} 7 \\ \times 6 \end{array}$

$3 \times 5 =$ $\begin{array}{r} 6 \\ \times 5 \end{array}$ $\begin{array}{r} 12 \\ \times 5 \end{array}$

$\begin{array}{r} 9 \\ \times 3 \end{array}$ $\begin{array}{r} 9 \\ \times 6 \end{array}$ $9 \times 12 =$

© Dale Seymour Publications

Arrays and Shares ■ 81

Help for You, the Teacher

Because we believe strongly that a new curriculum must help teachers think in new ways about mathematics and about their students' mathematical thinking processes, we have included a great deal of material to help you learn more about both.

About the Mathematics in This Unit   This introductory section (p. 11) summarizes for you the critical information about the mathematics you will be teaching. This will be particularly valuable to teachers who are accustomed to a traditional textbook-based curriculum.

Teacher Notes   These reference notes provide practical information about the mathematics you are teaching and about our experience with how students learn. Many of the notes were written in response to actual questions from teachers, or to discuss important things we saw happening in the field-test classrooms. Some teachers like to read them all before starting the unit, then review them as they come up in particular investigations.

Dialogue Boxes   Sample dialogues demonstrate how students typically express their mathematical ideas, what issues and confusions arise in their thinking, and how some teachers have guided class discussions.

These dialogues are based on the extensive classroom testing of this curriculum; many are word-for-word transcriptions of recorded class discussions. They are not always easy reading; sometimes it may take some effort to unravel what the students are trying to say. But this is the value of these dialogues: They offer good clues to how your students may develop and express their approaches and strategies, helping you prepare for your own class discussions.

Where to Start   You may not have time to read everything the first time you use this unit. As a first-time user, you will likely focus on understanding the activities and working them out with your students. Read completely through each investigation before starting to present it.

When you next teach this same unit, you can begin to read more of the background. Each time you present this unit, you will learn more about how your students understand the mathematical ideas. The first-time user of *Arrays and Shares* should read the following:

- About the Mathematics in This Unit (p. 11)
- Teacher Note: What About Notation? (p. 23)
- Teacher Note: The Relationship Between Multiplication and Division (p. 35)
- Teacher Note: Two Kinds of Division: Sharing and Partitioning (p. 51)

Teacher Checkpoints As a teacher of the *Investigations* curriculum, you observe students daily, listen to their discussions, look carefully at their work, and use this information to guide your teaching. We have designated Teacher Checkpoints as natural times to get an overall sense of how your class is doing in the unit.

The Teacher Checkpoints provide a time for you to pause and reflect on your teaching plan while observing students at work in an activity. These sections offer tips on what you should be looking for and how you might adjust your pacing. Are most students fluent with strategies for solving a particular kind of problem? Are they just starting to formulate good strategies? Or are they still struggling with how to start?

Depending on what you see as the students work, you may want to spend more time on similar problems, change some of the problems to use smaller numbers, move quickly to more challenging material, modify subsequent activities for some students, work on particular ideas with a small group, or pair students who have good strategies with those who are having more difficulty.

In *Arrays and Shares,* you will find two Teacher Checkpoints:

> Multiplication Clusters (p. 22)
> Choice Time (p. 44)

Embedded Assessment Activities Use the built-in assessments included in this unit to help you examine the work of individual students, figure out what it means, and provide feedback. From the students' point of view, the activities you will be using for assessment are no different from any others; they don't look or feel like traditional tests.

These activities sometimes involve writing and reflecting, at other times a brief interaction between student and teacher, and in still other instances the creation and explanation of a product.

In *Arrays and Shares*, you will find assessment activities in the second and third investigations:

> Creating and Solving Division Problems (p. 50)
> Solving Two-Digit Multiplication Problems (p. 68)

Teachers find the hardest part of the assessment to be interpreting their students' work. If you have used a process approach to teaching writing, you will find our mathematics approach familiar. To help with interpretation, we provide guidelines and questions to ask about the students' work. In some cases we include a Teacher Note with specific examples of student work and a commentary on what it indicates. This framework can help you determine how your students are progressing.

As you evaluate students' work, it's important to remember that you're looking for much more than the "right answer." You'll want to know what their strategies are for solving the problem, how well these strategies work, whether they can keep track of and logically organize an approach to the problem, and how they make use of representations and tools to solve the problem.

Ongoing Assessment Good assessment of student work involves a combination of approaches. Some of the things you might do on an ongoing basis include the following:

- **Observation** Circulate around the room to observe students as they work. Watch for the development of their mathematical strategies and listen to their discussions of mathematical ideas.

- **Portfolios** Ask students to document their work, in journals, notebooks, or portfolios. Periodically review this work to see how their mathematical thinking and writing are changing. Some teachers have each student keep a notebook or folder for each unit, while others prefer one mathematics notebook or a portfolio of selected work for the entire year. Take time at the end of each unit for students to choose work for their portfolios. You might also have them write about what they've learned in the unit.

Arrays and Shares

Content of This Unit Through the work in this unit—skip counting, building arrays, dividing quantities into equal shares, and solving word problems—students develop a clear sense of what multiplication and division are and how these processes are related. They use 100 charts, rectangular arrays, games, and cubes to gain fluency with multiplication and division pairs and to learn how to solve multiplication and division problems by breaking them into manageable components. Students are encouraged to develop their own strategies, based on what they know about numbers, for solving multiplication and division problems.

Students are asked to analyze real-world applications of multiplication and division situations and represent them mathematically to find solutions; they also create their own real-world problems for mathematical statements.

Connections with Other Units If you are doing the full-year *Investigations* curriculum in the suggested sequence for Grade 4, this is the second of eleven units. Your class will already have had some experience with skip counting on the 100 chart in the introductory unit, *Mathematical Thinking at Grade 4*. There, students looked for patterns on the 100 chart as they skip counted.

The work in this unit is also continued and extended in the Grade 4 units *Landmarks in the Thousands*, using larger numbers with factors and multiples of 100, and *Packages and Groups,* finding factors of larger numbers and solving multi-digit multiplication and division problems.

If your school is not using the full-year curriculum, this unit can also be used successfully in Grade 5.

Investigations Curriculum ■ Suggested Grade 4 Sequence

Mathematical Thinking at Grade 4 (Introduction)

▶ *Arrays and Shares* (Multiplication and Division)

Seeing Solids and Silhouettes (3-D Geometry)

Landmarks in the Thousands (The Number System)

Different Shapes, Equal Pieces (Fractions and Area)

The Shape of the Data (Statistics)

Money, Miles, and Large Numbers (Addition and Subtraction)

Changes Over Time (Graphs)

Packages and Groups (Multiplication and Division)

Sunken Ships and Grid Patterns (2-D Geometry)

Three out of Four Like Spaghetti (Data and Fractions)

Investigation 1 • Multiples on the 100 Chart			
Class Sessions	**Activities**	**Pacing**	
Sessions 1 and 2 MULTIPLES ON THE 100 CHART	Skip Counting on the 100 Chart Highlighting 100 Charts ■ Homework	2 hrs	
Session 3 SKIP COUNTING AND MULTIPLYING	Making Groups Solving Multiplication Clusters ■ Teacher Checkpoint: Multiplication Clusters ■ Homework	1 hr	

Investigation 2 • Arrays			
Class Sessions	**Activities**	**Pacing**	**Ten-Minute Math**
Session 1 THINGS THAT COME IN ARRAYS	Finding Arrays in and out of Our Classroom ■ Homework	1 hr	
Sessions 2 and 3 MAKING ARRANGEMENTS	Arranging a Group of 18 People Finding All Possible Arrays for a Number Class Discussion: Looking at All the Arrays ■ Extensions	2 hrs	
Session 4 MAKING A SET OF ARRAYS	Preparing a Personal Set of Array Cards Using the Array Cards	1 hr	Counting Around the Class
Sessions 5 and 6 ARRAY GAMES	Another Array Game Choice Time: Multiplying, Dividing, and Skip Counting ■ Teacher Checkpoint: Choice Time How Many Ways Can You Make 8 × 6? ■ Homework	2 hrs	
Sessions 7 and 8 LOOKING AT DIVISION	Introducing Division Notation Division Problems with Leftovers Class Discussion: Division with "Extras" ■ Assessment: Creating and Solving Division Problems ■ Homework	2 hrs	

Continued on next page

Investigation 3 • Multiplication and Division with Two-Digit Numbers

Class Sessions	Activities	Pacing	Ten-Minute Math
Session 1 MULTIPLICATION CLUSTERS	Solving Cluster Problems Writing About Your Strategies ■ Homework	1 hr	
Sessions 2, 3, and 4 MULTIPLICATION AND DIVISION CHOICES	Choice Time: Multiplication and Division Activities Class Discussion: Strategies for Solving Two-Digit Multiplication Problems Class Discussion: How Many Boxes Do You Need? ■ Homework	3 hrs	Multiple BINGO
Session 5 PROBLEMS THAT LOOK HARD BUT AREN'T	Discussing Multiplication Pairs Which Pairs Are Hard for You? Problems That Look Hard But Really Aren't ■ Assessment: Solving Two-Digit Multiplication Problems Choosing Student Work to Save ■ Homework	1 hr	

MATERIALS LIST

Following are the basic materials needed for the activities in this unit. The suggested quantities are ideal; however, in some instances you can work with smaller quantities by running several activities, requiring different materials, simultaneously.

Items marked with an asterisk are provided with the *Investigations* Materials Kit for Grade 4.

* Interlocking cubes: at least 50 per student pair
* Array Cards, Sets A and B (manufactured; or use blackline masters to make your own sets): 1 set per student

Calculators: at least 1 per student pair

Large poster or chart paper: 1 sheet per student pair

Construction paper (12" by 18"): 1 per student pair

Quart-size resealable plastic bags: 1 per student

Scissors, glue or paste, tape, crayons or markers

Overhead projector

The following materials are provided at the end of this unit as blackline masters. They are also available as classroom sets.

Family Letter (p. 80)

Student Sheets 1–10 (pp. 81–96)

Teaching Resources:

100 Chart (p. 97)

100 Chart (4 to a page) (p. 98)

One-Centimeter Graph Paper (p. 99)

Three-Quarter-Inch Graph Paper (p. 100)

How to Make Array Cards (p. 101)

Array Cards (pp. 102–118)

How to Play Multiplication Pairs (p. 119)

How to Play Count and Compare (p. 120)

How to Play Small Array/Big Array (p. 121)

Factor Cards (Ten-Minute Math) (p. 122)

This unit focuses on the process and application of multiplication and division. The multiplication and division situations in this unit deal with equal groups. Multiplication is used when the size of the group and the number of groups are known and we want to find the total number of items. Division is most often used when the total quantity is known and we are trying to find out either the number of groups or the size of the groups.

Traditional instruction in these important arithmetic processes emphasizes speed and memorization of single-digit "facts" and computation procedures. However, students may know their "facts" without being able to recognize situations in which multiplication and division are useful. They may learn procedures without having a sense of how multiplication and division really work.

The focus of this unit is on supporting students to make sense out of multiplication and division. As students develop strategies to use in multiplication and division situations, it is critical that they develop visual images that support their work. Through using an array model (a rectangular arrangement of objects in rows and columns), they begin to visualize important multiplication relationships, for example, that the solution to 7×6 is the same as the solution to 6×7. By combining arrays into larger arrays, they develop strategies to solve two-digit multiplication and related division problems. For example, the problem 7×23 can be solved by breaking the problem into more familiar parts: 7×10, 7×10, and 7×3.

Students need to develop efficient computation strategies, many of which will be mental strategies, but these must be based on their understanding of the quantities and their relationships, not on memorized procedures. Good mental strategies often start from the left, focusing first on the largest part of the number, rather than the smallest: For 56×8, we might think, "eight 50's is equal to 400, eight 6's is equal to 48, so that's 448." When students see standard notation for multiplication or division such as

$$\begin{array}{r} 56 \\ \times\ 8 \\ \hline \end{array} \qquad 8\,\overline{)\,432}$$

the form of the problem may trigger use of poorly understood, and often inefficient, algorithms. For example, in the first problem, students might start to say, "8 times 6 is equal to 48, put down the 8 and carry the 4." This procedure obscures the use of good number sense and often leads students to fragment a number into its digits and lose track of the quantities represented by the numerals. We would like students to recognize and interpret all the standard notations they are likely to see in elementary school but to continue to solve problems using good number sense and good strategies built on an understanding of the number relationships involved in the problem.

Mathematical Emphasis At the beginning of each investigation, the Mathematical Emphasis section tells you what is most important for students to learn about during that investigation. Many of these mathematical understandings and processes are difficult and complex. Students gradually learn more and more about each idea over many years of schooling. Individual students will begin and end the unit with different levels of knowledge and skill but all will gain greater understanding of multiplication and division situations and strategies for solving these problems based on good number sense and number relationships.

In the *Investigations* curriculum, mathematical vocabulary is introduced naturally during the activities. We don't ask students to learn definitions of new terms; rather, they come to understand such words as *factor* or *area* or *symmetry* by hearing them used frequently in discussion as they investigate new concepts. This approach is compatible with current theories of second-language acquisition, which emphasize the use of new vocabulary in meaningful contexts while students are actively involved with objects, pictures, and physical movement.

Listed below are some key words used in this unit that will not be new to most English speakers at this age level, but may be unfamiliar to students with limited English proficiency. You will want to spend additional time working on these words with your students who are learning English. If your students are working with a second-language teacher, you might enlist your colleague's aid in familiarizing students with these words, before and during this unit. In the classroom, look for opportunities for students to hear and use these words. Activities you can use to present the words are given in the appendix, Vocabulary Support for Second-Language Learners (p. 76).

packages, packaged Students examine items such as juice boxes and pencils, that are packaged or arranged in rectangular arrays. They look at the dimensions of these packages as one way of determining the total number of items. For example, eggs are usually packaged in 2 rows of 6 (2×6). Students could skip count by 2's as a way of determining the total number of eggs or they might add $6 + 6$ to figure the total.

related Students solve groups or clusters of multiplication problems that are related to each other. Some problems in the cluster might be related by doubles (4×5 and 4×10), or they might be multiples of 10 (3×2 and 3×20). Other problems might be broken down into smaller more familiar problems, such as 4×5, 4×10, and 4×15.

strategy, strategies Throughout the unit students are encouraged to share their ideas and approaches to solving problems. The emphasis is on solving problems and using ideas, processes, and strategies that make sense to the student. Students are encouraged to share their problem-solving strategies with their classmates. By doing this, students experience that there are many ways to solve a problem.

Multicultural Extensions for All Students

Whenever possible, encourage students to share words, objects, customs, or any aspects of daily life from their own cultures and backgrounds that are relevant to the activities in this unit. For example:

■ When students are making up problem situations that represent division situations, encourage them to write problems that are based on aspects of their cultures—foods, games, objects, and sports that involve teams, and so on.

Investigations

Multiples on the 100 Chart

What Happens

Sessions 1 and 2: Multiples on the 100 Chart
Students are introduced to skip counting on the 100 chart. They create a set of highlighted 100 charts that show the multiplication patterns of numbers. Students use these charts throughout the unit to practice skip counting and play games.

Session 3: Skip Counting and Multiplying
Students use interlocking cubes and skip counting on the 100 chart as tools for determining how many groups of a smaller number are in a larger number. They discuss how these problems can be represented using standard multiplication and division notation. They solve clusters of multiplication problems, using one solution to help them find others.

Mathematical Emphasis

■ Using skip counting as a model for multiplication (for example, count by 2's to see that six 2's is equal to 12)

■ Seeing multiplication as an accumulation of groups of a number (for example, use cubes or the 100 chart to show that 6 groups of 3 is equal to 18)

■ Looking for the multiplication patterns of numbers (including patterns of multiples highlighted on the 100 chart)

■ Interpreting standard multiplication and division notation

■ Using known multiplication relationships to solve harder relationships (for example, three 6's is equal to 18, so six 6's must be equal to 36 because 18 and 18 is equal to 36).

What to Plan Ahead of Time

Materials

- Markers or crayons for skip counting on the 100 chart (Sessions 1–2)
- Interlocking cubes: at least 50 per student (Session 3)
- Overhead projector (Sessions 1–3)

Other Preparation

- Duplicate Student Sheets and Teaching Resources (located at the end of this unit) in the following quantities:

For Sessions 1 and 2

100 chart (p. 97): 1 per student

100 chart (4 to a page) (p. 98): 4 per student; 1 for homework

Family letter (p. 80): 1 per student. Remember to sign it before copying.

For Session 3

Student Sheet 1, Multiplication Clusters: 1 per student

Student Sheet 2, More Multiplication Clusters: 1 per student (homework)

100 chart (p. 97): 1 per student (plus 1 for homework, optional)

- Assemble (or have the students assemble) interlocking cubes in towers of 10. Insist that students return cubes in groups of ten when they are finished using them.
- Make at least two overhead transparencies of the 100 chart (p. 97) (Sessions 1–3)
- If you plan to provide folders in which students will save their work for the entire unit, prepare these for distribution during Session 1.

Multiples on the 100 Chart

Materials

- 100 chart (1 per student, optional)
- 100 chart (4 to a page) (4 per student; 1 for homework)
- Markers or crayons
- Transparency of 100 chart
- Overhead projector
- Family letter (1 per student)

What Happens

Students are introduced to skip counting on the 100 chart. They create a set of highlighted 100 charts that show the multiplication patterns of numbers. Students use these charts throughout the unit to practice skip counting and play games. Their work focuses on:

- practicing skip counting
- looking for the multiplication patterns of numbers 2 to 12

Activity

Skip Counting on the 100 Chart

1	②	3	④	5	⑥	7	⑧	9	⑩
11	⑫	13	⑭	15	⑯	17	⑱	19	⑳
21	㉒	23	㉔	25	㉖	27	㉘	29	㉚
31	㉜	33	㉞	35	㊱	37	㊳	39	�40
41	㊷	43	㊹	45	㊻	47	㊽	49	㊿
51	52	53	54	55	56	57	58	59	60
61	62	63	64	65	66	67	68	69	70
71	72	73	74	75	76	77	78	79	80
81	82	83	84	85	86	87	88	89	90
91	92	93	94	95	96	97	98	99	100

Put a 100 chart on the overhead. Ask students which numbers would get circled if you were counting by 2's. Circle these numbers on the 100 chart. This is an appropriate time to integrate *multiple* as a word to describe the numbers you are circling. See the **Teacher Note**, Introducing Mathematical Vocabulary (p. 18).

It is not necessary to circle the numbers in order. In fact, skip around a bit—asking for some suggestions of multiples of 2 in the 40's or 70's. When you have a few multiples circled, ask some students or the whole class to count slowly in unison by 2's while you circle all the multiples of 2.

Finding Patterns   When all the multiples of 2 are circled or highlighted on the chart, have students describe the patterns they see for the 2's. Write down their observations on the chart.

Pass out 100 charts for students to highlight the multiples of 2. In addition to highlighting their charts, they should write one statement about a pattern they notice. As students finish, they can practice skip counting by 2's with a partner, using their highlighted 100 chart if they need it. One way to do this is for one student to look at the chart while the other counts without seeing the chart; the first student checks the count and provides hints as necessary.

Highlighting 100 Charts

Give each student four copies of the 100 chart (4 to a page). Each student makes highlighted 100 charts for the multiples of 2 to 12. Although each student makes his or her own set of charts, students should work in pairs or small groups.

As you circulate around the room, encourage students to check with one another continually; if they find differences, they need to figure out what to correct. Also, encourage conversations within groups about what patterns they see and what shortcuts they find in order to complete their charts.

At the bottom of each chart students should write a statement about the pattern they notice on the highlighted 100 chart.

❖ **Tip for the Linguistically Diverse Classroom** Have limited English proficient students circle a pattern they recognize for each 100 chart of multiples 2 to 12.

When students have finished a chart they should use their chart and practice skip counting by that number with a partner as a way of familiarizing themselves with the number sequence and checking the pattern on their 100 chart. Skip counting can be confusing for some students, and it is also quite easy to make an error. See the **Teacher Note**, Students' Problems with Skip Counting (p. 19), for some issues to watch out for and ideas about how to support students who might have difficulty.

Sharing Patterns Pose some questions about the group of charts for the class to investigate:

Are there charts that have only even numbers?

Are there charts that have only odd numbers?

What numbers never seem to be highlighted? Why do you think that is true? On what other charts might they be highlighted?

What else did you notice?

Students can staple their pages of 100 charts together and keep them in their math folders to refer to as needed. As they become more familiar with the patterns of the multiples of 2 to 12, they will probably use their charts less and less. Since these charts are useful for reference throughout the year, some teachers have had their students make them into more permanent books with sturdy covers.

Sessions 1 and 2 Follow-Up

🏠 Homework

Send the family letter home today with one copy of the 100 chart, 4 to a page. Assign students two or three charts to complete at home. They may complete two or three charts for either multiples of 2 to 12 that they did not complete in class or multiples of numbers such as 15 and 16. Remind them to write one statement about a pattern they notice for each completed chart. If possible, they can practice skip counting with an adult or sibling.

Teacher Note ▷ *Introducing Mathematical Vocabulary*

This unit provides the opportunity for introducing several important mathematical words naturally. Introduce these words by beginning to use them yourself and explaining what you mean by them, but don't insist that students use them. If the introduction of a vocabulary word is preceded by activities that make its definition clear, students enjoy knowing an "adult" word to refer to a new concept they have learned.

Multiple *Multiple* is a natural word to introduce to students as they count by 2's (or any other number) and circle those numbers on the 100 chart. During the activity refer to the numbers you have circled as "the multiples of 2." You might ask students if they have other names for these numbers, such as "the 2's table" or "counting by 2's."

Factor A *factor* of a number is a number that can be divided evenly into another number. For example, 2 is a factor of 4, 6, 8, and all the even numbers; 1, 2, 4, 8, and 16 are all factors of 16. The idea of factors comes up naturally when students make and use arrays. The dimensions of each array are factors of the total number in the array.

Even and Odd These words will come up in the students' descriptions of patterns on the 100 chart. Don't assume that students know exactly what they mean by these words. Some children believe that an even number has only even factors: "No, 3 isn't a factor of 24 because 3 isn't even." This is a good conjecture to have students investigate.

Row and Column When talking about their ways of working with the 100 chart, students often confuse the words *row* and *column,* describing a pattern as going "down the row" rather than "down the column." This may be a good opportunity to talk about the difference, since using *row* for both (as students often do) makes communication more difficult. However, do not insist that students use these words in the conventional way as long as they can explain or demonstrate what they mean. Remembering the difference can be honestly confusing, and focusing on getting the words right may obscure the good mathematical thinking a student is doing. Rather, keep using them yourself so students continually hear them used correctly in context. Other terms that may come up in this context and may need some explanation are *horizontal, vertical,* and *diagonal.*

Students' Problems with Skip Counting

Some students have difficulty keeping track of their count on the 100 chart. Here are some confusions we have noticed in classrooms:

- Students sometimes start on 1, no matter which number they are skip counting by.

- Students' count is off by 1 because they start counting with the last number they circled. For example, when counting by 6's, a student counts 6, 12, 18, and then begins his or her next count on 18, counts six numbers (18, 19, 20, 21, 22, 23), and lands on 23 instead of 24.

- Students follow a "false pattern" that doesn't actually work for the number they are counting by. For example, some students circle 3, 6, 9, and then color straight down the columns under the 3, 6, and 9, not realizing the 3's pattern doesn't continue in columns like the 2's pattern does.

- Students miscount one interval and then continue counting correctly so that all the subsequent numbers are affected by the original mistake—for example: 3, 6, 9, 12, 15, 19, 22, 25, 28, and so on.

Some of these difficulties are simply the kind of miscounting mistakes anyone can make. Help students use the pattern on their 100 charts to check: Does the pattern continue consistently on the chart? Also, have students double-check one another. When two or three students compare charts, they can often find and correct their own miscounting.

However, some students may truly not understand what they are doing when they "count by 2's" or "count by 3's" on their charts. These students can build their 2's or 3's with cubes first. A student makes a group of 2 cubes, then marks 2 on the 100 chart; then makes another group of 2 cubes (perhaps in a different color), and then marks the total, 4; then makes another group of cubes, marks the total 6; and so forth. Allow students to stop using the cubes as soon as they feel comfortable.

We have found that it is not helpful for students to use cubes to mark squares directly on the 100 charts. Students can't see the numbers underneath them, and they often move a cube accidentally to a neighboring square, thereby misleading themselves about the pattern on the chart.

Skip Counting and Multiplying

Materials

- Interlocking cubes (at least 50 per student)
- 100 chart (1 per student)
- Transparency of 100 chart
- Student Sheet 1 (1 per student)
- Student Sheet 2 (1 per student, homework)
- 100 chart (1 per student, homework, optional)

What Happens

Students use interlocking cubes and skip counting on the 100 chart as tools for determining how many groups of a smaller number are in a larger number. They discuss how these problems can be represented using standard multiplication and division notation. They solve clusters of multiplication problems, using one solution to help them find others. Their work focuses on:

- representing multiplication
- interpreting multiplication and division notation
- solving related multiplication problems
- skip counting

Activity

Making Groups

Make sure all students have access to interlocking cubes. Pose the following question to students as a way of connecting the idea of "counting by 2's" to accumulating groups of 2's.

Using your cubes, show how many 2's it would take to make 24.

Circulate quickly as students are building to check that they can demonstrate that it takes 12 groups of 2 to make 24.

How could you show the same thing on your 100 chart? Is there a way to use the chart to show that 12 groups of 2 make 24?

Take time to explore this question. You may need to follow up with questions, such as:

How many groups of 2 have you counted when you skip count to 4? to 12? How can you tell from the chart?

Pose another, related problem:

How many 2's are in 48?

After students talk with a partner about this problem for a minute or two, ask them to present their solutions. Students might solve this problem using cubes, using the 100 chart, or relating this problem to the previous one.

Using Standard Multiplication and Division Notation Ask students how they would write down "24 groups of two make 48" with numbers or with words. Record their suggestions:

24 groups of 2 make 48 $2 + 2 + 2 + 2 + ... = 48$

$$24 \times 2 = 48$$
$$\begin{array}{r} 24 \\ \times\, 2 \\ \hline 48 \end{array}$$

If no one suggests the standard multiplication notation, $24 \times 2 = 48$, introduce it yourself and read it as "24 groups of 2 is equal to 48." Show students that it can be written vertically or horizontally.

Note: At this point, you might want to introduce or students might bring up the related division problems:

$$48 \div 2 \qquad 2\overline{)48} \qquad 48 \div 24 \qquad 24\overline{)48}$$

Students might read the first two problems as "How many 2's are in 48?" or "Divide 48 into 2 parts." We will focus on interpreting division notation in Investigation 2.

Solving Multiplication Clusters

Write a cluster of related problems on the board using the 3's chart. As students look at their charts, ask them to solve these problems and explain their solutions:

$$3 \times 3 \qquad 6 \times 3 \qquad \begin{array}{r} 12 \\ \times\ 3 \\ \hline \end{array}$$

Encourage students to use facts they know or have just solved to help them with the related problems:

How can knowing that 3 × 3 is equal to 9 help you to solve 6 × 3? How does the solution to 6 × 3 help you with 12 × 3? If you have 6 groups of 3 cubes in front of you, how many more groups will you have to make in order to have 12 groups? How many cubes would that be?

Don't worry if not all students are able to use these strategies right away; they will have many more opportunities in this unit to work on these kinds of relationships.

Tell students they will be working on "clusters" of multiplication problems they can solve using their 100 charts or cubes. The problems are arranged in such a way that if you figure out one of the facts, it may help you find a clever strategy to solve some of the others in the cluster. Refer to any strategies students discovered for the previous problem.

Teacher Checkpoint

Multiplication Clusters

Students work in pairs on Student Sheet 1, Multiplication Clusters. As you circulate, make sure students can prove their solutions using the 100 charts or cubes and can interpret the multiplication problems meaningfully as, for example, "12 groups of 4" or "twelve 4's." If students say something like "It's 48 because 4 times 2 is equal to 8 and 4 times 1 is equal to 4" for 12 × 4, it is likely that they are seeing individual digits and are losing the meaning of this expression as "12 groups of 4." Your role in supporting students to interpret written notation meaningfully is absolutely critical (see the **Teacher Note**, What About Notation?, p. 23). Students may think about a problem such as 4 × 12 as "12 groups of 4" or "4 groups of 12." Either of these interpretations is reasonable. The relationship between the two interpretations will be explored further in Investigation 2 (for more about this issue, see the **Teacher Note**, The Relationship Between Multiplication and Division, p. 35).

Send home Student Sheet 2, More Multiplication Clusters, for homework. Suggest to students that they find something at home to count with (such as pennies or paper clips) or they might want to bring home a blank 100 chart.

🏠 Homework

What About Notation?

Teacher Note

It is important that your students learn to recognize, interpret, and use the standard forms and symbols for multiplication and division, both on paper and on the calculator. In this unit, students will use these:

$$12 \qquad 3 \times 12 \qquad 12 \div 3 \qquad 3\overline{)12}$$
$$\underline{\times\ 3}$$

Your challenge is to introduce these symbols in a way that allows students to interpret them meaningfully. That is, students must understand what is being asked in a problem that is written in standard notation. They can then devise their own way to find an answer. Notation is also useful as an efficient way to record a problem and its solution. It is not just a directive to carry out a particular procedure, or a signal to forget everything you ever knew about the relationships of the numbers in the problem!

Your students may come to you already believing that when they see a problem like $3\overline{)42}$, written in the familiar division format, they must carry out the traditional long-division procedure. Instead, we want them to use everything they know about these two numbers in order to solve the problem. They might skip count by 3's out loud or on the calculator. (For tips on skip counting on the calculator, see the Ten-Minute Math activity, p. 73.) Or they might use reasoning based on their understanding of number relationships:

It takes ten 3's to make 30. Then there are three more 3's to get up to 39, that's thirteen 3's so far. Then 40, 41, 42—that's one more 3—it's 14!

Well, half of 42 is 21, and I can divide 21 into seven groups of 3, so you double that, and it's 14.

Similarly, when students see a multiplication problem like 4 x 55 written vertically, they are likely to forget everything they know about these numbers and try to carry out multiplication with carrying. Instead, we want students to use what they know about landmarks in the number system and other familiar number relationships. For example:

I know that two 50's make 100, and there's four 50's, so that's 200. Then I know that four 5's is 20, so it's 220.

Students need to get used to interpreting multiplication in both horizontal and vertical form as simply indicating a multiplication situation, not a particular way to carry out the problem. So, while you help students to read standard notation and to use it to record their work, keep the emphasis on understanding the problem context and using good number sense to solve the problem.

INVESTIGATION 2

Arrays

What Happens

Session 1: Things That Come in Arrays
Students think of items that are packaged or arranged in arrays (a rectangular arrangement of objects in rows and columns), such as juice cans or window panes. They record these types of arrays, their dimensions, and the total number of items.

Sessions 2 and 3: Making Arrangements Using cubes and graph paper, students make all the possible arrays for a number. They make a poster of all the arrays, labeling the dimensions of each. Students discuss what they have observed about the class set of posters and explore prime and composite numbers.

Session 4: Making a Set of Arrays Students make a personal set of array cards for use throughout the remainder of the unit. They cut out the array cards in Set A, outlined in the Teaching Resources, consisting of 51 arrays, which represent the multiplication combinations of the factors 2 through 12 with totals (or products) up to 50. Later in the unit, or as they become fluent working with these cards, students gradually add the larger arrays in Set B. Students begin to learn several games that use the array cards.

Sessions 5 and 6: Array Games During these two sessions, students are introduced to Choice Time. They have the opportunity to play three array games and to practice skip counting in pairs or small groups. As they become more comfortable and familiar with these arrays, they add larger numbers to their sets until the sets represent all multiplication combinations with factors 2 through 12.

Sessions 7 and 8: Looking at Division Students are introduced to division and division notation through word problems that represent various types of division situations. They explore the relationship between the situations and the standard notations and decide how to solve problems in which the solutions do not come out evenly.

Mathematical Emphasis

■ Using an array as a model for multiplication (for example, a gridded rectangle or array that is 3 units by 5 units models the multiplication problem 3 × 5)

■ Becoming more familiar with multiplication problems

■ Becoming comfortable with a variety of notations used for multiplication and division (in addition to the symbols ×, −, ÷, and =, students may use a multiplication symbol to represent a division situation and vice versa)

■ Recognizing prime numbers as those that each have only one pair of factors and only one array

■ Understanding how division notation represents a variety of division situations (including sharing situations and partitioning situations)

■ Determining what to do with "leftovers" in division, depending on the situation (for example, rounding the quotient up or down or expressing the "leftovers" as a remainder, a fraction, or a decimal)

What to Plan Ahead of Time

Materials

- Interlocking cubes: at least 50 per pair (Sessions 1–8)
- Large poster or chart paper to make a class list of arrays (Session 1)
- Construction paper (12" by 18"): 1 per student (Sessions 2–3)
- Scissors, glue, paste, tape (Sessions 2–4)
- Manufactured Array Cards, Sets A and B, provided in the grade 4 Materials kit: 1 set per pair (optional) (Sessions 4–8)
- Quart-size resealable plastic bags to hold array cards: 1 per student (Sessions 4–8)
- Calculators: at least one per pair (Sessions 7–8)
- Overhead projector (Sessions 1, 4–8)

Other Preparation

- Duplicate Student Sheets and Teaching Resources (located at the end of this unit) in the following quantities:

For Session 1

Student Sheet 3, Things That Come in Arrays: 3 per pair, 1 per student for homework

Three-quarter-inch graph paper (p. 100): 1–2 per pair

For Sessions 2 and 3

Three-quarter-inch graph paper (p. 100): 2–3 per pair

For Sessions 4, 5, and 6

Array Cards, Sheets 1–6, Set A

(pp. 102–107): 1 set per student (if you haven't purchased the grade 4 Materials kit)

Array Cards, Sheets 7–17, Set B (pp. 108–118): 1 set per student (if you haven't purchased the grade 4 Materials kit)

How to Make Array Cards (p. 101): 1 per student

Game Directions for the three array games (pp. 119–121) (You may want to make copies to post in the classroom and one copy for each student to take home.)

For Sessions 7 and 8

Student Sheet 4, What Do You Do with the Extras?: 1 per student

Student Sheet 5, What's the Story?: 1 per student

Student Sheet 6, Word Problems: 1 per student

- Look for things arranged in arrays that you can bring in to show the class, such as an egg carton, a package of buttons, or a page from a calendar (Sessions 1–2).
- Clear space to display the students' array posters (Sessions 2–3).
- Familiarize yourself with the rules of the three array games (Sessions 4–8).
- Make an overhead transparency of Student Sheet 3 for Session 1.
- Make overhead transparencies of Array Cards, Sheets 1–6 (pp. 102–107). Then cut out each of the 51 arrays for Sessions 4–8.

Things That Come in Arrays

Materials

- Interlocking cubes (at least 50 per pair)
- Poster or chart paper to make a class list of arrays
- Student Sheet 3 (3 per pair, 1 for homework)
- Transparency of Student Sheet 3
- Three-quarter-inch graph paper

What Happens

Students think of items that are packaged or arranged in arrays (a rectangular arrangement of objects in rows and columns), such as juice cans or window panes. They record these types of arrays, their dimensions, and the total number of items. Their work focuses on:

- using arrays as models for multiplication
- using skip counting to count arrays
- relating multiplication notation to arrays

Ten-Minute Math: Counting Around the Class Once or twice during the next few days, do Counting Around the Class. Remember, Ten-Minute Math activities are done outside math time in any spare 10 minutes you have.

Choose a number to count by, let's say 3. Ask students to predict what number they'll land on if they count by 3's around the class exactly once. Encourage students to talk about how they could figure this out without doing the actual counting.

Then start the count: The first student says "3," the next "6," the next "9," and so forth. Encourage students to use their 100 charts if they need to. As students learn the sequence of counting by different numbers, they will rely less on their charts and more on their knowledge of the counting pattern.

Stop two or three times during the count to ask a question like this:

We're at 33. How many students have counted so far?

After counting around once, compare the actual ending number with students' predictions.

For full instructions and variations, see p. 72.

Finding Arrays in and out of Our Classroom

Groups of things often come in rectangular arrays. Imagine a six-pack of juice cans. How many rows do you see? How many cans are in each row? Does anyone see it differently?

Students may describe this array as either three rows of two cans or two rows of three cans.

On the board or an overhead begin a chart where you can write the name of the item, write how many total items are in the array, write the dimensions of the array (written in both ways), and draw the array in both orientations. Here's a format you could use (or use a transparency of Student Sheet 3, Things That Come in Arrays):

Things That Come in Arrays

Item	Total	Dimensions		Arrays
six-pack of juice cans	6	2 rows of 3 3 rows of 2	2 × 3 3 × 2	
eggs	12	2 rows of 6 6 rows of 2	2 × 6 6 × 2	
yogurt containers	4	2 rows of 2	2 × 2	
thumbtacks	100	10 rows of 10	10 × 10	

❖ **Tip for the Linguistically Diverse Classroom** Show the following items as they are discussed: a six-pack of juice cans, eggs, yogurt containers, and thumbtacks.

What other things can you think of that come in rectangular arrays? Think about the way food is packaged at the grocery store.

What things in this room are in arrays? (window panes, cubbies, tiles, groupings of desks)

Write down some of the students' ideas on your chart. Begin to use the word *dimensions* naturally, just as you have introduced other mathematical terms into the dialogue with your class. Describe the arrays as "3 by 2" or "4 by 3," so students become used to hearing this language.

Students then work in pairs to fill in Student Sheet 3, Things That Come in Arrays (students may need several copies). Some students may need to represent their items with cubes, tiles, or centimeter paper in order to record all the information. As you watch students work, encourage them to count their arrays using skip counting, not by ones.

Things That Come in Arrays

Item	Total	Dimensions	Draw the Array
6-pack of juice cans	6	2 rows of 3 2 x 3 3 rows of 2 3 x 2	
eggs	12	2 rows of 6 2 x 6 6 rows of 2 6 x 2	
yogurt containers	4	2 rows of 2 2 x 2	
thumbtacks	100	10 rows of 10 10 x 10	

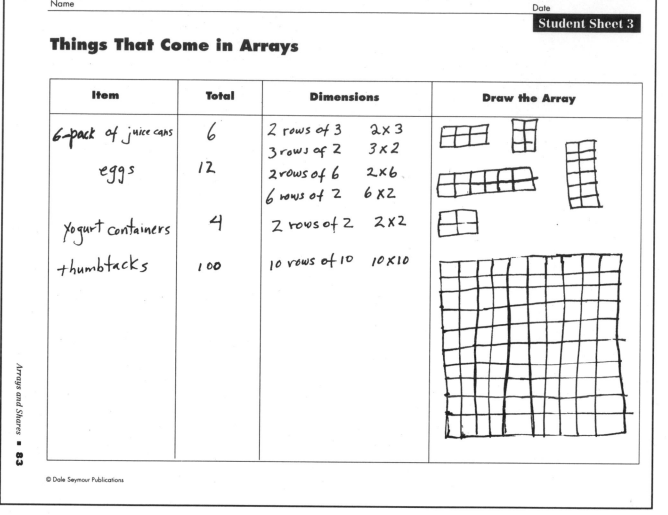

Leave 10 minutes at the end of the session for students to share their find-ings. On chart or poster paper, begin a class list of the items students have thought of, along with the dimensions. After you have recorded several items, you might ask the following:

What items are packaged in the same types of arrays? Which arrays seem to be most popular?

What items have the same number of objects along each side? (For example, 10 × 10)

How are these arrays different from other arrays?

Throughout the rest of the unit, students can continue to search for new arrays and add them to the class list.

Students look for arrays at home and record them on a copy of Student Sheet 3. Some students may want to bring in arrays to show the class. As students arrive at school tomorrow, have them add to the class list new arrays they have found.

❖ Tip for the Linguistically Diverse Classroom To ensure comprehension for all students, encourage everyone to bring in actual examples of the arrays listed on their charts if they can.

🏠 **Homework**

Making Arrangements

Materials

- Class array list from previous session
- Interlocking cubes (at least 50 per pair)
- Three-quarter-inch graph paper (2–3 per pair)
- 12" by 18" construction paper (1 per student)
- Scissors, glue, paste, tape

What Happens

Using cubes and graph paper, students make all the possible arrays for a number. They make a poster of all the arrays, labeling the dimensions of each. Students discuss what they have observed about the class set of posters and explore prime and composite numbers. Their work focuses on:

- finding factors of numbers
- recognizing prime numbers as numbers with only one pair of factors
- using an array as a model for multiplication

Activity

Discussing Homework

As students arrive at school today, have them add to the class list the new arrays they found for homework. Spend some time discussing these new arrays (see the **Dialogue Box**, Things That Come in Arrays, p. 36).

What are the totals that seem to be most common? Were there any numbers smaller than 20 that you didn't find any items for? Why do you suppose that is?

Make lists of items that come in the most common amounts. List each item under the total amount.

12	3	4
eggs	tennis balls	yogurt containers
ice cubes	cupcakes	tires
pencils		

Encourage students to keep looking for arrays, especially for numbers for which no one has yet found examples.

. . . .

❖ **Tip for the Linguistically Diverse Classroom** Instead of making a list, have limited English proficient students group the items brought from home by their total amounts. Then have them identify which piles are representative of items that come in the most common amounts.

. . . .

Arranging a Group of 18 People

When a group of people need to sit down, we often arrange chairs in an array that fits the space. Can you think of some of the places this happens? (movie theater, bus, airplane, school auditorium)

How could we arrange chairs in a rectangular array for a group of 18 people? How else might 18 chairs be arranged in an array?

Students, working in pairs, use interlocking cubes to make all the arrays they can for 18. Ask each group to choose one of their arrays and cut it out from the graph paper.

Make sure each possible array for 18 is represented. Collect a sample of each array for 18 from the students and post them where all can see them. Some students will see 3 × 6 and 6 × 3 as two different arrays; others will think of them as the same (see the **Teacher Note**, The Relationship Between Multiplication and Division, p. 35). Allow students to discuss their ideas about this. We suggest that you put up both arrangements, posting pairs next to each other. Arrays provide a model that helps students visualize how multiplication pairs, such as 3 × 6 and 6 × 3, are related. (If you put up all the pairs, you should have 6 arrays: 1 × 18, 18 × 1, 2 × 9, 9 × 2, 3 × 6, and 6 × 3.)

Ask students to help you label the arrays. This is a good time to establish a class convention for which arrays will be labeled 3 × 6 (3 rows of 6) and which will be labeled 6 × 3 (6 rows of 3). A convention will help students and you communicate with one another more clearly; however, it is less important that students use the convention consistently than that they can clearly demonstrate what they mean.

Counting Squares in Arrays   Ask students for their ideas about ways to count one of the arrays, for example, the 3 by 6 array. Some students will count the arrays by 1's, counting each individual square. Other students will see that a 3×6 array can be counted by 3's (3, 6, 9, 12, 15, 18) or by 6's (6, 12, 18). Sometimes students come up with more inventive ways, such as seeing a 3×6 as consisting of two 9's. Emphasize counting by groups by having students look at other arrays for 18. As students make arrays for other numbers in the next activity, continue to encourage them to count their arrays by groups.

Finding All Possible Arrays for a Number

During the second half of Session 2 and most of Session 3, each student works with a partner on finding ways to arrange different-size groups.

We suggest students make arrays for the following size groups: 10, 14, 15 through 30, 32, 36, 40, 42, 44, 45, 48, 49, and 50. Either assign to each pair of students one of these numbers to work on or write the numbers on squares of paper and let students choose the number they would like. List on the chart or overhead the numbers that students have chosen as a way of keeping track of which numbers have been done. Students can use interlocking cubes to help them plan their arrays. Students should find all the possible arrays for their number and cut out each array from the two-centimeter graph paper. They glue the arrays onto a larger piece of construction paper to create a "poster" for each number with a title such as "Ways to Make 24." They should label each array with its dimensions.

Talk with groups as you observe them working:

How can you know when you have found all the arrays for one number?

Have you found any numbers that have only one array?

How can you count your array to make sure the total is correct?

Encourage students to use more than one way of counting, in order to double check the total (see the **Dialogue Box**, A Short Way to Count, p. 37). As students finish, ask them how they know they have all the arrays for their number. Encourage students to look for ways of checking their arrays by listing them in an organized way, such as 1×36, 2×18, 3×12, 4×9, 6×6. Students can post finished posters on the wall and choose another number from the list to work on. If all the numbers have been done, suggest that they choose another number (under 50) they would like to investigate.

Since students will need to see the arrays for the discussion at the end of this session, it's important to choose a place to post them where they can be viewed by all students.

Class Discussion: Looking at All the Arrays

Near the end of these two sessions, set aside about 20 minutes for students to view all the arrays, to make observations about the arrays, and to discuss, as a class, what they've noticed as they worked on their array posters. In pairs, students walk around to view all the array posters and jot down at least two discoveries they have made about the arrays in general. You might want to start their thinking by saying:

As you walk around and look at the arrays, here are some things you might pay attention to: How many arrays does each number have? Can you find out anything about even and odd numbers? See if you can make some discoveries by looking at all our arrays.

In a class discussion, students share and discuss these discoveries. Make a list of students' observations about the arrays they've constructed. Students might notice:

Some numbers have only two arrays (for example, 13 × 1 and 1 × 13). Some students might say these numbers just have one array (since the two are really the same one in a different orientation). Another way to describe these numbers is that they have only two factors, 1 and the number itself. These special numbers are called *prime numbers*. What prime numbers have students found? Do they know any above 50? Numbers having more than two arrays—or more than two factors—are called *composite numbers*.

Since arrays come in pairs (for example, 3 × 4 and 4 × 3), most numbers have an even number of arrays.

A few numbers have an odd number of arrays. This occurs when one of the arrays is a square (for example, 10 × 10), which does not have another orientation. Some students may recognize that these numbers, such as 16, 25, and 36, are the *square numbers*.

Odd numbers never have arrays with even dimensions, but some even numbers have arrays with both even and odd dimensions. Why is this true? Why don't odd numbers sometimes have arrays with even dimensions?

Ask students: Which of your observations do you think is always true? Which observations do you need to keep testing as you look at arrays for other numbers?

Keep the list of their observations posted so it can be added to or revised during the course of the unit.

Sessions 2 and 3 Follow-Up

 Extensions

■ **Arrays for Higher Numbers** Some students may be interested in finding the arrays for higher numbers. Interesting numbers for students to investigate include 56, 60, 64, and 72.

■ **Prime Numbers** Students can also find the prime numbers from 1 to 100. This is a good activity in which to integrate the calculator.

The Relationship Between Multiplication and Division

Multiplication and division are related operations. Both involve two factors and the multiple created by multiplying those two factors. For example, here is a set of linked multiplication and division relationships:

$$8 \times 3 = 24 \qquad 3 \times 8 = 24$$
$$24 \div 8 = 3 \qquad 24 \div 3 = 8$$

Mathematics educators call all of these "multiplicative" situations because they all involve the relationship of factors and multiples. Many problem situations that your students will encounter can be described by either multiplication or division. For example:

I bought a package of 24 treats for my dog. If I give her 3 treats every day, how many days will this package last?

The elements in this problem are: 24 treats, 3 treats per day, and a number of days to be determined. This problem could be written in standard notation as either division or multiplication:

$$24 \div 3 = \underline{\quad} \qquad \text{or} \qquad 3 \times \underline{\quad} = 24$$

Once the problem is solved, the relationships can still be expressed either as division or multiplication:

24 treats divided into 3 treats per day results in 8 days ($24 \div 3 = 8$)

3 treats per day for 8 days is equivalent to 24 treats ($3 \times 8 = 24$)

Many students in the elementary grades are more comfortable with multiplication than with division, just as they are often more comfortable with addition than with subtraction. We want students to recognize and interpret standard division and multiplication notation. However, we do not want to insist that they use one or the other to record their work when both provide good descriptions of a problem situation. In the dog-treat problem, either notation is a perfectly good description of the results.

Similarly, the order of the factors doesn't matter when describing a multiplication situation. Both of the examples that follow provide good descriptions of the dog-treat problem:

3 treats per day for 8 days is equivalent to 24 treats ($3 \times 8 = 24$) (3 per group in 8 groups is 24 total)

8 days with 3 treats per day is equivalent to 24 treats ($8 \times 3 = 24$) (8 groups with 3 per group is 24 total)

While some people prefer one or the other way to write these factors, we do not feel that a standard order (either putting the number of groups first or the number in each group first) should be taught or insisted upon. As long as students can explain their problem and their solution and can relate the notation clearly to the problem, the order of the factors in multiplication equations is not critical.

D I A L O G U E   B O X

Things That Come in Arrays

Students are discussing the new arrays they found for homework (p. 30).

I want to show you what Sara brought in. [*The teacher holds up an egg carton.*] **What can you tell me about this?**

Nick: It's an egg carton.

Marci: It's a 3 by 6.

Pinsuba: It can hold 18 eggs.

B.J.: You could say it has 6 rows of 3 or 3 rows of 6.

I have another egg carton over there on the table. How would you describe that one?

Kenyana: A 2 by 6.

What else can you say about it?

Kyle: Or a 6 by 2.

Irena: It holds 12.

Lesley Ann: It's like a dozen.

What do you mean by a dozen?

Lesley Ann: It's 12. A dozen is the same as 12.

Alex: My dad says a baker's dozen is 13.

How can you compare these two arrays?

Joey: Both hold eggs.

Sarah: Both count by 6's.

Kim: One's bigger.

Rebecca: One just has 6 and 6. The other one has 6 and 6 and 6.

What if I do this? (The teacher tears the egg carton for a dozen in half.)

Nick: That's a 2 by 3.

How many eggs does it hold?

Jesse: Six.

Rikki: Half a dozen.

David, want to share your album? What's it for?

David: Basketball cards. Each page is a 3 by 3.

How many cards will it hold?

David: Nine to a page, and I have almost 5 pages full.

Emilio: He'll have 45 if he gets 5 pages, because 9, 18, 27, 36, 45— that's five 9's.

Did anyone else find a different array?

Nhat: An ice tray.

Tell us about the ice tray.

Nhat: It's a 7 by 3. It has 21 holes.

That's an unusual ice tray with three rows. Any other arrays? [*Many students call out and the sharing continues.*]

This discussion takes place while students are working on the activity Finding All Possible Arrays for a Number (p. 32).

David: I made arrays for 24 people. One of my arrays was 6 by 4. I just thought 6 and 6 is 12, then I could see that was half of my array and just knew 12 and 12 was equal to 24.

Tyrone: You could also say 6, 12 ,18, 24. That's counting each row of 6.

Are there any other ways of counting David's array?

Shoshanna: You could count it by 4's too, but I think that takes longer than counting by 6's.

How would you count to 24 by 4's?

Tyrone: You know—4, 8, 12, 16, 20, 24.

Luisa: The 12 by 2 array is easy to count because there are 2 rows of 12, and 12 and 12 is equal to 24.

David: You could always count by 2's—2, 4, 6, 8, all the way to 24.

Shoshanna: Hey, it kind of seems like there's a short way to count and a long way. See, counting by 12's you just say 2 numbers, and counting by 2's you say a lot more. Same with 6's and 4's.

How many numbers do you have to say when you count by 2's?

[*Some students quickly count by 2's on their fingers, some look at their 100 charts, some count by 2's with cubes.*]

Making a Set of Arrays

Materials

- Quart-size resealable plastic bags (1 per student)
- Scissors
- Student Sheet 4 (1 per student)
- Array Cards, Sheets 1–6, Set A (1 set per student)
- Array Cards, Sheets 7–17, Set B (1 set per student)
- How to Make Arrays (1 per student)
- Transparencies of Array Cards, Sheets 1–6 (optional, for demonstrating students' ideas)

What Happens

Students make a personal set of array cards for use throughout the remainder of the unit. They cut out the array cards in Set A, outlined in the Teaching Resources, consisting of 51 arrays, which represent the multiplication combinations of the factors 2 through 12 with totals (or products) up to 50. Later in the unit, or as they become fluent working with these cards, students gradually add the larger arrays in Set B. Students begin to learn several games that use the array cards. Their work focuses on:

- using an array as a model for multiplication
- becoming more familiar with multiplication pairs

Activity

Preparing a Personal Set of Array Cards

Tell students they are going to make a set of array cards for multiplication pairs. They will use the cards to play games and to practice multiplication problems. During the first few days, students will use arrays for totals up to 50 (Array Cards, Set A). As they become more comfortable with these pairs they can add in arrays for totals up to 144 (Array Cards, Set B).

If you have the Array Cards provided in the grade 4 Materials kit, students can use these during class. However, each student will need an individual paper set, made from the Array Cards sheets in the Teaching Resources, for homework assignments.

Give each student a set of Array Cards, Sheets 1–17, scissors, and a quart-size resealable plastic bag to hold the cut-apart arrays. Introduce the process of cutting out and labeling the cards as a whole-class activity. Then give students a copy of How to Make the Arrays, and let them finish making their array cards independently.

Explaining the Procedure After carefully cutting out an array, students label the grid side of the card with the dimensions of the grid (for example, 6 × 4, 4 × 6). On the other side of the card (the blank side), students label the total number of squares in the grid. They may also label one dimension lightly in pencil, as a hint to help them when the arrays are new. They can erase this hint when they feel more confident. **Note:** Students should label their arrays with pencil, not magic marker or crayon, so the numbers cannot be seen through the paper.

<table>
<tr><td></td><td></td><td></td><td></td><td></td><td></td></tr>
<tr><td></td><td>6</td><td>×</td><td>4</td><td></td><td></td></tr>
<tr><td></td><td>4</td><td>×</td><td>6</td><td></td><td></td></tr>
<tr><td></td><td></td><td></td><td></td><td></td><td></td></tr>
</table>

```
         6

    24
```

Students will use their sets of arrays throughout this unit and in the unit *Packages and Groups* later in the year. They should label them with their initials and store them in the plastic bags.

Activity

Using the Array Cards

Students use their array cards to play two multiplication and division games, Multiplication Pairs and Count and Compare. Directions for these games are available in the Teaching Resources (pp. 119–120). The **Teacher Note**, Array Games, on p. 40, highlights the kinds of skills emphasized by these games.

The games can be taught to the whole class or to small groups of students. To begin you might teach the Multiplication Pairs game to pairs of students after they complete their array cards. These students can then teach other students.

Ten minutes before the end of this session have the students stop working so that you can introduce the Count and Compare game to the whole class. You can play this game on the overhead or by taping array cards to the board. As you demonstrate the game, ask students for ideas about how the arrays can be counted. Encourage students to count by groups, looking at the number of squares in a row or column. Ask students if they can determine which array has a bigger total by comparing the dimensions of two arrays.

Suppose you were comparing two arrays and did not know the total of either array. How could looking at the dimensions of the arrays help you decide which one was bigger? What if the length of one array is bigger than the other but the width is less? How might you compare the two to determine which array had the most squares?

Most students need to place the arrays next to each other or on top of each other to match the sides and count the squares that overhang.

If there is time, let the students play a few rounds of Count and Compare in pairs. During the next two sessions and in the next investigation students will have time to play these array games and learn others.

Teacher Note ▷ *Array Games*

Students use their sets of arrays to play multiplication and division games over the course of many days. Using the arrays in this way gives students a variety of opportunities to use a concrete model for multiplication and division, and in the process of playing the games, they become more familiar with the "multiplication pairs."

The Multiplication Pairs game focuses on practicing the problems by representing them as rectangular arrays. By looking at the dimensions (for example, 8 × 6), students can skip count the rows or columns or do repeated addition to figure the total amount. When they look at the total (48) they need to think about the possible multiplication combinations (4 × 12 or 6 × 8) that make 48, and select the combination that best matches the dimensions of the rectangle. They are often thinking of division here: "I know I can skip count by 4's to 48; let's see, how many 4's is it?" By recording the pairs they know and don't know, students keep track of their own progress and can be encouraged to set reasonable goals for learning new multiplication pairs.

The game Count and Compare provides students with opportunities to compute in a variety of ways the total number of squares in an array. Some students may choose to skip count the rows in order to figure the total. Some students will know just certain pairs and not need to figure the total. Other students might look at the

dimensions of the two arrays, comparing the length of rows and columns. Because there are various ways to count and compare the arrays, this game allows students with varying experience with multiplication and division pairs to play together. You might need to establish some guidelines—for example, each person has to compute his or her own total—as a way of allowing each student the time and opportunity to think about each array.

The Small Array/Big Array game encourages students to build a larger array from two or three smaller arrays. By doing this, they create a concrete model for how a multiplication situation such as 7 × 9 can be pulled apart into smaller, more manageable components, such as 3 × 9 and 4 × 9. As they record each match in the form of an equation, they connect the concrete model with the equations that represent these relationships.

All students should have the opportunity to play each game more than once during the course of this unit. Having students play array games in pairs keeps the pace of the game moving. As students play the games and use their arrays, they become more familiar with the multiplication and division pairs each array represents. They play the games during Investigations 2 and 3 and should take their paper set of arrays home to play with family members for homework.

Array Games

What Happens

During these two sessions students are introduced to Choice Time. They have the opportunity to play three array games and to practice skip counting in pairs or small groups. As they become more comfortable and familiar with these arrays, they add larger numbers to their sets until the sets represent all multiplication combinations with factors 2 through 12. Their work focuses on:

■ becoming more familiar with multiplication and division pairs through arrays and skip counting

Ten-Minute Math: Counting Around the Class Once or twice during the next few days, continue to do Counting Around the Class.

Count by 4's or 5's. Before you begin, ask:

If we count by 4's (or 5's) around the class do you think that the number we end on will be more or less than 100? Why do you think that?

Stop two or three times during the count and ask questions like these:

We're at 65 now, how many students have counted?

How many more students will have to have turns before we reach 100?

On some days you might have everyone use a calculator or have a few students use calculators to skip count while you are counting around the class.

For full instructions and variations, see p. 72.

Materials

■ Array Cards, Set A (1 set per pair)

■ Array Cards, Set B (1 set per pair)

■ Array Game Directions

■ Highlighted 100 charts from Investigation 1

■ Overhead projector

■ Transparencies of Array Cards, Sheets 1-6

Activity

Another Array Game

Begin today's session by introducing the Small Array/Big Array game. (Directions for this game can be found in the Teaching Resources, p. 121.) You can introduce this game to the entire class by playing with a small group of students, or you can teach the game to one group of students at a time while the others play one of the array games introduced in the last session. Because this game is played on a flat surface, you might want to gather the students in a circle on the floor or around a group of desks to demonstrate.

Display all the arrays. Ask students to find two arrays that could be used to "match" a bigger array. For example:

If you are trying to cover a 5 × 7 array and have a 2 × 7 array, what array would you need to complete the match?

As "matches" are completed, ask students to express the match using mathematical notation and check it by comparing the totals of the smaller arrays with the bigger array. For example, in the above situation, students would write: 5 × 7 = 2 × 7 + 3 × 7; this checks because 35 = 14 + 21.

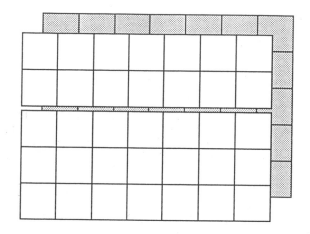

Once students grasp the idea of this game, allow them to play with partners. Students alternate finding matches.

Activity

Choice Time: Multiplying, Dividing, and Skip Counting

Four Choices For the remainder of this session and the next, students choose from four multiplication and division activities going on simultaneously in the classroom. This is referred to as Choice Time. This format allows students to explore the same idea at different paces. Students may repeat an activity, using different numbers or problems. You might want to establish an expectation with your students that they play at least two array games and practice skip counting with their partners by the end of tomorrow's session. Many students will have extra time and may choose to play all of the array games or just one game many times.

These activities are designed to give students more experiences using models, such as the 100 chart, and arrays to help them develop their knowledge of the multiplication and division relationships.

How to Set Up the Choices Write the four choices on the board with a list of the materials needed for each choice, as a reminder for the students.

If you set up your choices at stations, list the materials students will find at each station. Students can keep track of their choices on their own choice lists.

Choice 1: Array Game: Multiplication Pairs: directions; Array Cards, Sets A and B (1 set per pair)

Choice 2: Array Game: Count and Compare: directions; Array Cards, Sets A and B (1 per pair)

Choice 3: Array Game: Small Array/Big Array: directions; Array Cards, Sets A and B (1 set per pair)

Choice 4: Skip Counting: students' highlighted 100 charts from Investigation 1

Introduce Choice 4, Skip Counting, which is described below. Choices 1, 2, and 3 are array games with which the students are already familiar. Make copies of game directions available or simply post each sheet. Students may refer to the directions when in doubt about the rules of the game. Students may choose to play using only the Array Cards in Set A, which consists of multiplication pairs with products up to 50. Then when they feel comfortable, students may include Array Cards from Set B.

Choice 1: Array Game: Multiplication Pairs

Given the dimensions of an array, students are to find the total number of squares in the array; given the total, students are to find the dimensions. As they play, students write the multiplication pairs and relationships they know and don't know on a sheet of paper.

Choice 2: Array Game: Count and Compare

Students use multiplication relationships to find the sizes of students' array cards and then determine the largest.

Choice 3: Array Game: Small Array/Big Array

Students use their array cards to make "matches" between a large array and two or more smaller arrays. Each student should write their "matches" on a sheet of paper using mathematical statements.

Choice 4: Skip Counting

With a partner, students practice skip counting by 2's through 12's, using the highlighted 100 charts they made in Investigation 1, if they need to. One way to do this is for one student to look at a chart while the other student counts without seeing the chart; the first student checks the count and provides hints as necessary. You might suggest that students who choose this activity skip count by 2's, 3's, and 6's and write down these and other numbers they do on their choice list.

Teacher Checkpoint

Choice Time

During Choice Time, circulate among the groups and observe students as they are involved with an activity, or use the time to meet with small groups of students who are having difficulty with a particular activity.

Some things you might look for are the following:

- How are students making decisions about choosing an activity and organizing their time and materials?
- Are there too many or not enough activities going on at once?
- Are students keeping track of the choices they have completed?
- How are students figuring out the total number of squares in arrays? Are they counting one by one? Counting by groups? Do they know the multiplication pairs?
- Do some students need to spend more time counting by 2's, 3's, and 6's?
- Are some students ready to add the next set of arrays (Set B) to their existing set?

Students will continue working on all the activities throughout the next investigation.

Some students may need help in making choices and keeping track of what they need to do and what they have completed during Choice Time. It will probably take a few sessions before students are feeling more confident with the routines and expectations. You may ask for student volunteers to act as resources for classmates who need help or clarification.

You can make adjustments in the number of choices offered, the number of array cards that students work with, and the overall pacing of Choice Time in order to best meet the needs of your classroom.

How Many Ways Can You Make 8 × 6?

At the end of Session 6, bring the class together for a discussion about the Small Array/Big Array game. Students will need their sets of array cards.

As you played Small Array/Big Array, what clues helped you decide which two smaller arrays might match up to make a bigger array?

Let's take a look at the 8 × 6 array. What are some of the combinations of smaller arrays that would equal this array? Use your set of arrays to make as many 8 × 6 arrays as you can using either two or three arrays.

Every student or student pair builds 8 × 6 arrays on their desks. When most students have constructed a few examples, ask students to share their combinations of arrays by describing the dimensions of the smaller arrays. Record these on the board or overhead as shown below. If you have made a set of overhead arrays, you can display the examples as well as record the dimensions.

Challenge students to find all the ways to make 8 × 6 using two arrays. If you record combinations in an ordered list such as the one below, students may more easily use the patterns to exhaust all possible combinations.

8 × 6 = 7 × 6 + 1 × 6   8 × 6 = 8 × 1 + 8 × 5
   48 = 42 + 6   48 = 8 + 40

8 × 6 = 6 × 6 + 2 × 6   8 × 6 = 8 × 2 + 8 × 4
   48 = 36 + 12   48 = 16 + 32

8 × 6 = 5 × 6 + 3 × 6   8 × 6 = 8 × 3 + 8 × 3
   48 = 30 + 18   48 = 24 + 24

8 × 6 = 4 × 6 + 4 × 6
   48 = 24 + 24

Here are the ways to construct 8 × 6 using two arrays:

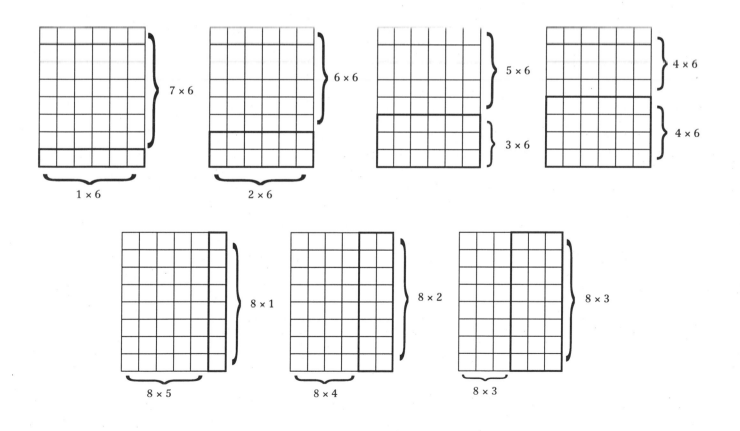

Emphasize the idea that unfamiliar multiplication situations can be broken down into smaller, more manageable components:

If you don't know how much 12 × 4 is equal to, how could you break it down into more familiar parts that you know?

Sessions 5 and 6 Follow-Up

🏠 **Homework**

Students play Multiplication Pairs, Small Array/Big Array, or Count and Compare at home. Students can either take their array cards home or use copies of the Array Cards, Sheets 1 to 17, together with the directions for making array cards to make a set of cards for home. Some students may also want a copy of the directions for each game.

Note: If students' paper sets are the only array cards you have, they must remember to bring them back to school each day during the course of the unit!

Looking at Division

What Happens

Students are introduced to division and division notation through word problems that represent various types of division situations. They explore the relationship between the situations and the standard notations and decide how to solve problems in which the solutions do not come out evenly. Their work focuses on:

- recognizing division situations
- using division notation
- solving division problems
- expressing remainders using problem context

Materials

- Array Cards
- Calculators
- Student Sheet 4 (1 per student)
- Student Sheet 5 (1 per student)
- Student Sheet 6 (1 per student, homework)

Ask students to get out all the arrays that have 36 total squares. Write on the board:

36 ÷ 4

Here's a division problem. How do you read this? Which array would help you solve it?

Creating Problems   Students create their own problem situations to model the above division expression.

Can you think of a problem situation that you'd write down as 36 ÷ 4?

Students may think of division problems that involve sharing ("There are 36 marbles being shared among 4 friends. How many marbles will each person get?") and division problems that involve grouping or measuring ("There are 36 marbles. I'm going to put 4 marbles in each bag. How many bags will I need?"). See the **Teacher Note**, Two Kinds of Division: Sharing and Partitioning (p. 51) for more information about these two division situations.

Activity

Introducing Division Notation

Introduce the notation: $4\overline{)36}$

Discuss with students how this is read, and point out the total that is being divided appears as the second number, whereas when they use the ÷ notation, it is the first number. (See **Teacher Note**, Talking and Writing About Division, p. 53.)

How would you use your calculator to solve this problem? Which keys would you use? Which number would you put in first?

Students try to solve the problem on their calculators and share their strategies and solutions.

Creating More Problems Ask students to look at their arrays to find other ways to divide 36.

How else can you divide up 36? Who can think of a new problem situation that involves dividing up 36?

Students spend a few minutes working in pairs to generate division problems that start with the total 36. Have them:

1. Write down each problem situation (for example, "There are 36 children who are going to divide up into 6 teams for relay races. How many will be on each team?").

2. Write down the notation for that problem using both ÷ and $\overline{)}$.

3. Give the solution to their problem ÷ and $\overline{)}$.

As you circulate, observe whether students are comfortable creating division problems and whether they understand the correspondence between their problem situation and the written notation. Help students to read notation in context; for example, the expression $36 \div 9$ may be read as "36 divided into 9 groups" in a sharing situation or as "how many 9's are in 36?" in a partitioning situation.

Ask some students to present their problems. Other students can demonstrate how to express the problems using standard notation and can give the solutions.

Division Problems with Leftovers

Write on the chalkboard:

$36 \div 5$

Look at this problem. What would be a situation in which you would have 36 divided by 5?

List students' answers on the board. Then using students' situations to illustrate this problem, discuss how you would find the solution to $36 \div 5$ and what would happen to the "extra." Students may express this extra as a fraction, a decimal, or a remainder or leftover amount.

Have students work in groups on Student Sheet 4, What Do You Do with the Extras? Tell students that these are all division problems where you can't divide the total evenly. Their job is to decide what to do in each case and to write down their reasoning and a reasonable solution. Students can use their arrays and calculators.

Class Discussion: Division with "Extras"

Ask students to share their solutions to the division problems on Student Sheet 4. Invite some students to write their solutions with explanations on the board. Sample solutions may include:

There are 36 people to be transported in vans that hold 8 people. How many vans do you need?

> There are 4 vans with 4 people left.
> So you'd need 5 vans to take all the people.

There are 36 crackers that will be shared by 8 people. How many crackers will each person get?

> Each person can get 4 crackers. Keep 4 crackers for another day.
> $36 \div 8 = 4$ crackers per person with 4 extras
>> or
> Each person can get $4^{1}/_{2}$ crackers. $36 \div 8 = 4^{1}/_{2}$

There are 36 people in rows of 8. How many rows will you need?

> There are 32 people who will fit in 4 rows. Then 4 people have to sit in row 5. $36 \div 8 = 4$ rows, with 4 more people
>> or
> You fill up 4 rows and half of another row. $36 \div 8 = 4.5$

Assessment: Creating and Solving Division Problems

Students work individually on Student Sheet 5, What's the Story? Explain that students are to think of a division situation for each of the expressions on the student sheet. As you observe students working and look at their finished papers, consider the following:

1. Does this student understand what kinds of situations are represented by written division notation? Does this student include both sharing and grouping situations in the problems?

2. Can this student solve division problems accurately? Does the student use the array cards or the calculator appropriately to solve these problems? Can the student do many of these division problems mentally?

3. Can this student give a reasonable solution when the total cannot be divided evenly into equal groups?

4. Is this student able to use fractions or decimals appropriately in the solution to Problem 2 (and Problem 4)?

❖ **Tip for the Linguistically Diverse Classroom** Have limited English proficient students use pictures or drawings to convey their story problems.

After Session 8, students may take home Student Sheet 6, Word Problems, to complete as homework.

 Homework

Two Kinds of Division: Sharing and Partitioning

Teacher Note

There are two distinct kinds of division situations. Consider these two problems:

> I have 18 balloons for my party. After the party is over, I'm going to divide them evenly between my sister and me. How many balloons will each of us get?

> I have 18 balloons for my party. I'm going to tie them together in bunches of 2 to give to my friends. How many bunches can I make?

Each of these problems is a division situation—a quantity is broken up into equal groups. The problem and the solution for each situation can be written in standard notation as $18 \div 2 = 9$.

Although similar, these two situations are actually quite different. In the first situation, you know the number of groups—2. Your question is, "How many balloons will be in each group?" In the second situation, you know that you want 2 balloons in each group, and your question is, "How many groups will there be?" In each case you divide the balloons into equal groups, but the results of your actions look different.

I have 18 balloons and 2 people. How many for each person?

I have 18 balloons to put in bunches of 2. How many bunches?

Continued on next page

The first situation is probably the one with which your students are most comfortable, because it can be solved by dealing out. That is, the action to solve the problem might be: one for me, one for you, one for me, one for you, until all the balloons are given out. In this situation, division is used to describe sharing.

In the second situation, the action to solve the problem is making groups—that is, taking out a group of 2, then another group of 2, and another, and so on, until no balloons are left. In this situation, division is used to describe *partitioning*.

Students need to recognize both of these actions as division situations and to develop an understanding that both can be written in the same way: 18 ÷ 2 = 9. Therefore, in this unit we present both kinds of division problems and, depending on the situation, help students interpret the notation as either "How many 2's are in 18?" or "Divide 18 into 2 groups; how many in each group?"

As students become more flexible with division, they will understand that they can think of a sharing situation as partitioning, or a partitioning situation as sharing, in order to make it easier to solve. For example:

How many will be in each team if I make 25 teams from 100 people?

To solve this, I will probably not deal out 100 into 25 groups. It is easier to think, "How many groups of 25 are in 100?"—knowing that the answer to this partitioning question will also give me the answer to the sharing problem I need to solve. Some of your students may soon have an intuitive understanding that they can divide in either way to solve a division problem.

Also, as students get more experience with both multiplication and division, they will begin to recognize how related problems can help them. Just as 2 × 9 = 9 × 2, 18 ÷ 2 = 9 is already related to 18 ÷ 9 = 2. When you find students stuck in routines that are difficult to keep track of—such as dealing out 100 into 25 teams—ask if thinking about a similar problem might help them. "If there were 100 people in all and 25 people on a team, how many teams would there be? Does that give you any ideas about making 25 teams from 100 people?"

Talking and Writing About Division

Various division symbols are used as standard notation in our society:

$$24 \div 4 \qquad 4\overline{)24}$$

$$24/4 \qquad \frac{24}{4}$$

We want students to recognize these forms (which they may see on tests and in other textbooks) as having the same meaning. They will use the fractional form in the Fractions units of the *Investigations* curriculum.

There are many different ways to "read" or speak of these notations:

Four goes into (or, as students say, "guzinta") 24

24 divided by 4

How many 4's are in 24?

When 24 is shared among 4 people, how many does each person get?

So many symbols and so many different ways of reading them can be very confusing to young students, especially because the numbers and symbols appear in different positions, depending on which notation you are using. We would like students to read division notation with as much meaning as possible, so that they connect the symbols to the situations they represent.

The first two ways (above) of "reading" these notations correspond to the ways the symbols are written, and may seem simpler to you. However, "Four goes into 24" is a phrase that carries little meaning about the division operation. Encourage students to interpret these symbols as "24 divided into 4 parts, or "How many 4's are in 24?" These two phrases express more meaningfully what the notation represents.

Talk explicitly with your students about what these symbols mean, and how it can be confusing to read them. Work with them to help them remember that the quantity being divided is always the first number in the form $24 \div 4$, and always the inner number in the form $4\overline{)24}$. Don't let them rely on thinking of the bigger number

as the one being divided, since $1 \div 2$ (for example) is a perfectly legitimate division problem, in which a smaller number is divided by a larger number.

Sometimes a problem does not divide evenly. Rather than teaching students to write "R" for the remainder, have them describe the remainder in any way that makes sense to them for that problem. For example, how many groups of 3 can be formed with 26 students? Some students may decide they can make 8 groups of 3 and one group of 2. Others may decide to make 6 groups of 3 and two groups of 4. If the example was 26 cookies to share among 3 children, they might give 8 to each and leave the remaining 2 cookies on the plate, or break them up to share.

For more about helping students connect their own good strategies with standard notation, see the **Teacher Note**, What About Notation? (p. 23).

Multiplication and Division with Two-Digit Numbers

What Happens

Session 1: Multiplication Clusters Students solve groups ("clusters") of related multiplication problems. They look for patterns and relationships within each cluster that can help them solve the problems and then write about their problem-solving strategies.

Sessions 2, 3, and 4: Multiplication and Division Choices Students choose from a selection of multiplication and division activities, including array games, skip counting, and solving multiplication clusters, and division word problems.

Session 5: Problems That Look Hard But Aren't In the final session of this unit, students work in small groups to generate a list of "hard"

multiplication pairs (or relationships). The class compiles a list of these pairs and discusses which are the most difficult to learn and which they have developed strategies for solving. They solve a two-digit multiplication problem as a whole class. As an assessment activity, students solve another two-digit problem in two different ways.

Mathematical Emphasis

- Partitioning numbers to multiply them more easily (for example, 7×23 can be 7×10 plus 7×10 plus 7×3)

- Recognizing multiplication and division situations and representing each situation using a mathematical statement

- Learning about patterns that are useful for multiplying by multiples of 10 (multiplying by 10, 20, ..., 100)

What to Plan Ahead of Time

Materials

- Interlocking cubes: at least 50 per student (Sessions 1–5)
- Array Cards, Sets A and B: 1 per student

Other Preparation

- Duplicate Student Sheets and Teaching Resources (located at the end of this unit) in the following quantities:

For Session 1

One-centimeter graph paper (p. 99): 1–2 per pair

For Sessions 2-4

One-centimeter graph paper (p. 99): 1–2 per pair

Student Sheet 7, Multiplication Clusters, Sets A–L: 1 per student

Student Sheet 8, Problems About Our Class: 1 per student

Student Sheet 9, Recycling Problems: 1 per student

For Session 5

One-centimeter graph paper (p. 99): 1–2 per student pair

Student Sheet 10, Two Ways to Solve a Problem: 1 per student

- Photocopy and post directions to Array Games: Big Array/Small Array, Multiplication Pairs, and Count and Compare (pp. 119–121).
- Duplicate the 100 Chart (p. 97) (1 per student) and the Factor Cards (p. 122). (1 set per pair) for the Ten-Minute Math: Multiple BINGO.

Multiplication Clusters

Materials

- Interlocking cubes
- One-centimeter graph paper (1–2 per pair)

What Happens

Students solve groups ("clusters") of related multiplication problems. They look for patterns and relationships within each cluster that can help them solve the problems and then write about their problem-solving strategies. Their work focuses on:

- using multiplication relationships
- breaking down large problems

Activity

Solving Cluster Problems

Introduce students to what a cluster problem is and explain why you are doing them.

For the next few days we'll be thinking about good strategies for figuring out hard multiplication problems. We'll be looking at groups of multiplication problems that are related to one another. These groups of problems are called Cluster Problems. You can work on the problems in any order. You can use the interlocking cubes or the graph paper to make arrays to help you solve these problems.

Present the following cluster:

$$4 \times 5$$
$$4 \times 10$$
$$5 \times 4$$
$$4 \times 15$$

Students talk with group members about how to solve this first cluster. They can work on the problems in any order.

When they have finished, have volunteers show how they did the problems to the whole class.

When students are ready, present another cluster of similar problems.

$$2 \times 8$$
$$8 \times 1$$
$$8 \times 10$$
$$12 \times 8$$

Students complete the problems and compare strategies within their groups. As the students are working, circulate among the groups and note the strategies students are using.

Sharing Strategies Bring the whole class together briefly to share strategies they have figured out for themselves or learned from one another. Possible questions you might ask to help focus their thinking are:

Did you learn something useful from someone else in your group? Tell us about it.
In what order did you solve the problems?
Did anyone solve them in a different way?
Did you learn anything from one problem that helped you solve another problem?

Writing About Your Strategies

Show a third set of problems that are similar in format. Suggest to students they try to solve mentally any problems they can and just write down the answers, then use these answers to solve the other problems.

$$3 \times 10$$
$$3 \times 20$$
$$3 \times 4$$
$$3 \times 24$$

This time, students work alone to solve the problems. They write about how they did it and illustrate the strategies by drawing arrays or cutting them out of centimeter graph paper and pasting them on their papers.

❖ **Tip for the Linguistically Diverse Classroom** Have limited English proficient students demonstrate their thought processes by illustrating their strategies as shown in the example on this page. Omit instructions that direct students to write about their approach.

One way to solve 3 × 24 is with centimeter graph paper:

The **Dialogue Box,** Ways to Solve 3 × 24 (p. 60), gives some examples of student strategies for solving multiplication clusters.

Session 1 Follow-Up

Homework

Assign a set of cluster problems such as the following:

7 × 3
7 × 10
7 × 6
7 × 16

Students find the solution to each problem and write about how they did the problems. Provide time in the next session for students to compare their solutions and strategies with neighboring classmates. Encourage students to invent their own set of cluster problems they can exchange with classmates.

❖ **Tip for the Linguistically Diverse Classroom** Have limited English proficient students demonstrate their solutions by illustrating their strategies as shown in the example on this page. Omit the instructions that direct them to write about their approach and to invent their own set of cluster problems.

Cluster Problems

Students are provided with clusters of three or four related multiplication problems and asked to find and use the relationships that exist to solve the problems. The cluster problems used in this investigation are designed to help students make sense out of multiplying and dividing with two-digit numbers and to help them gain a sense of what happens when you multiply a number by 10 or 100. We want them to build an understanding of the process by pulling apart numbers into manageable pieces, that is, 10's and 20's, and then multiplying the pieces. We want students to see that 9×23 can be thought of as $9 \times 10 + 9 \times 10 + 9 \times 3$ or that they can think about 9×23 as 10×23 minus a group of 23. Encouraging students to "use what they know"

to figure these problems is central. We hope they will construct a real sense of multiplying (and later dividing) by 10 and 100, not just memorize the pattern of adding zero and applying it as an algorithm.

As students write about how they solve cluster problems, it provides the teacher with some insight into their problem-solving strategies and how they are thinking about multiplicative relationships. Initially students should be encouraged to say how they solved 9×3 ("I counted by 9's," "I knew that 9 plus 9 is equal to 18, then added 9 more"). As they become more familiar with the multiplication pairs they should be encouraged to commit more of them to memory.

SET C

$2 \times 5 = 10$

$3 \times 5 = 15$

$10 \times 5 = 50$

$30 \times 5 = 150$

$32 \times 5 = 160$

on the last one I knew that 30×5 =150
So I did
$5 \times 2 = 10$
$30 \times 5 = 150$
$150 + 10 = 160$

SET E

$3 \times 5 = 15$

$10 \times 5 = 50$

$20 \times 5 = 100$

$23 \times 5 = 115$

We knew the first three. For the last one we did 20×5+3×5.

SET D

$5 \times 7 = 35$

$10 \times 7 = 70$

$2 \times 7 = 14$

$20 \times 7 = 140$

$25 \times 7 = 175$

On the last one I knew that 20×7=140 So I did 5×7=35
$20 \times 7 = 140$
$140 + 35 = 175$

SET F

$3 \times 6 = 18$

$3 \times 10 = 30$

$6 \times 10 = 60$

$3 \times 60 = 180$

$60 \times 3 = 180$

We knew the first one. With the third answer, you double the second. The last one was the reverse of the 4th one.

▪ D I A L O G U E ▪ B O X ▪

Ways to Solve 3 × 24

The class has been working on the following cluster problem in the activity *Writing About Your Strategies* (p. 57). They have written about how they have solved the cluster and are sharing their strategies for thinking about 3 × 24 in a whole-class discussion.

> 3 × 10
>
> 3 × 20
>
> 3 × 4
>
> 3 × 24

Kumiko: The way I did these was to count by each number. For 3 × 10, I counted by 10's. For 3 × 20, I counted by 20's. I just knew 3 × 4 was equal to 12. Then for 3 × 24, I added three 24's.

Rafael: I knew that 3 × 20 was 60 from the second problem. I knew that 3 × 4 was equal to 12, then I added the two together and got 72.

Ahmad: The way I figured out 3 × 24 was I know 24 plus 24 is equal to 48, so I added 2 from the next 24 and that made 50. Then I had to add the 22 that was left to the 50, and this gave me 72.

Shoshana: At first I didn't know how to do 3 × 24, but I knew that 3 × 20 = 60. So I tried to add 4 to the 20 and that made 24, *[Shoshana wrote 3 × 24 = 60]*. Then I added 4 to the 60 and got 3 × 24 = 64. But now I can see I made a mistake because I should have added three 4's to 60, not just one.

Vanessa: Mine was sort of like Ahmad's way. I just knew that 24 plus 24 is equal to 48, then I added 24 more and got 72.

Joey: I counted by 24's: 24, 48, 72!

Nick: I took 60 from 3 × 20, then I added 4 more 3's and got 72.

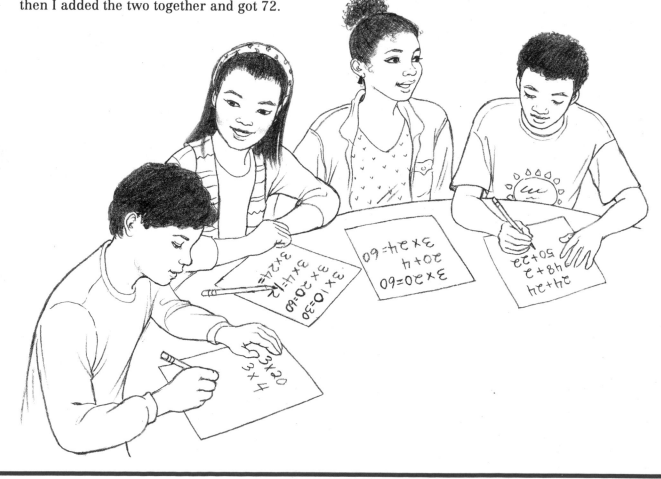

Multiplication and Division Choices

What Happens

Students choose from a selection of multiplication and division activities, including array games, skip counting, and solving multiplication clusters and division word problems. Their work focuses on:

■ recognizing multiplication and division situations

■ using multiplication and division notation

■ solving multiplication and division problems

 Ten-Minute Math: Multiple BINGO During the next few days, have students spend time outside of math class playing Multiple BINGO. Remember that Ten-Minute Math activities are best done outside of math time.

Using 100 charts, students try to color in 5 numbers in a row.

A factor card is turned over from the deck, and each player may color in any multiple of that factor on the 100 chart.

If a player turns over a Wild Card, that player decides what factor it represents. For a full description of Multiple BINGO, see the game directions on p. 74.

Materials

■ Array Cards, Sets A and B (1 set per student)

■ Interlocking cubes

■ One-centimeter graph paper

■ Student Sheet 7, Sets A–L (1 set per student; Sets K–L for homework)

■ Student Sheet 8 (1 per student)

■ Student Sheet 9 (1 per student)

■ Game Directions

Choice Time: Multiplication and Division Activities

Six Choices During Sessions 2, 3, and 4 of this investigation, students may choose from the six multiplication and division activities listed on page 62. Students may have worked on the first four of these activities in Choice Time: Multiplying, Dividing, and Skip Counting (p. 42). If you and your students have not done a Choice Time before, it will be important to establish some guidelines during this session.

How to Set Up the Choices Either distribute a blank Choice List to each student or have students use their own paper. Introduce the six activities and have students list them as you go over each. You might write the six choices on the board as a reminder for the students. If you set up your choices at stations, show students what materials they will find at each station.

Choice 1: Skip Counting: students' highlighted 100 charts from Investigation 1

Choice 2: Array Game: Small Array/Big Array: directions; Array Cards, Sets A and B (1 set per pair)

Choice 3: Array Game: Count and Compare: directions; Array Cards, Sets A and B (1 set per pair)

Choice 4: Array Game: Multiplication Pairs: directions; Array Cards, Sets A and B (1 set per pair)

Choice 5: Multiplication Clusters: Student Sheet 7: directions and multiplication clusters, Sets A–J (1 complete set per student)

Choice 6: Solving Division Word Problems: Students Sheet 8, Problems About Our Class (1 per student); and Student Sheet 9, Recycling Problems (1 per student)

Briefly explain to students what you expect them to do in order to complete each choice. For example, you might establish that during the next three sessions each student should play Multiplication Pairs twice, each student should do three to four multiplication clusters, or each student should skip count with a partner and do three to four division problems. Tell students they may do more if they have time.

Choices 1 to 4

For Choices 1 through 4, you can find a description of the activity in Choice Time: Multiplying, Dividing, and Skip Counting (p. 42). At this time, most students should be ready to use the Array Cards in Set B.

Choice 5: Multiplication Clusters

The directions for this activity are found on Student Sheet 7, page 1 of 7. In this activity, students work with a partner to solve multiplication problems.

Students choose two or three multiplication cluster sets from Student Sheet 7 to discuss with their partners. They talk about strategies for finding the answers to each problem.

Each student chooses one of their clusters and writes the solution and strategy used to solve each problem in the cluster. Partners may choose the same cluster set or different sets to write about. Then partners proofread each other's writing for clarity.

Choice 6: Solving Division Word Problems

Students work in pairs or small groups to solve division problems. Students may choose from problems found on Student Sheet 8, Problems About Our Class, and Student Sheet 9, Recycling Problems. For each problem, students should write an equation using division notation that represents the problem and then write how they solved the problem or draw a picture.

❖ **Tip for the Linguistically Diverse Classroom** Pair limited English proficient students with English proficient students to do the problems on Student Sheets 8 and 9. Ask English proficient students to make the words comprehensible to their partners by reading each problem aloud, and by pointing to objects in the classroom or drawing a picture as they read key words.

Making Choices Students may initially need help in making choices. Those students who have decided on their first choice can independently begin their work. Some students may need your help in deciding which choice they want or need to go to. It will probably take a few choice sessions before students are feeling more confident with these routines and expectations.

While Students Are Working on the Choices

During these sessions you might want to work with a small group of students who are having difficulty with specific choice items. Enlist the help of students who understand choice items to act as "resources" or "helpers" for their peers who might have questions.

During today's Choice Time, I'm going to be working with a small group of students on Multiplication Clusters. If you think you would like to work on this choice or if you feel like you're not really understanding how to do Multiplication Clusters, come join us. If you have a question or need some help during Choice Time, you might ask a friend for some help. Is there anyone who feels that he or she understands Division Word Problems or Small Array/Big Array and would be willing to help someone who has a question?

Discussing Choice Activities At some point during these three sessions, have two class discussions. One discussion should focus on students sharing their strategies for solving a set of multiplication clusters (Set D, Student Sheet 7, page 3 of 7) and the other on a division word problem (Problem 2, Student Sheet 9). Both problems are from the student sheets they have been working on during Choice Time. Prior to each discussion, remind students to complete each of these problems. More detail about the discussions is given on pp. 64 and 65.

Class Discussion: Strategies for Solving Two-Digit Multiplication Problems

The focus of this discussion is for students to share their strategies for solving two-digit by one-digit multiplication problems. As students share their ideas, listen for evidence suggesting students are using patterns that are useful, for example, multiplying by multiples of 10, partitioning larger numbers into smaller components, and viewing multiplication as groups of things.

Put this multiplication cluster on the board or overhead:

$$5 \times 7 =$$
$$10 \times 7 =$$
$$2 \times 7 =$$
$$20 \times 7 =$$
$$25 \times 7 =$$

Here's a multiplication cluster you have been working on during Choice Time. What are some of the ways you solved this cluster?

Encourage students to think about which multiplication pairs or relationships they "just knew" versus those pairs where they utilized skip counting or some other strategy. Students don't need to elaborate on how they solved single-digit multiplication problems if they have become automatic.

In a multiplication cluster, how does knowing the answer to one problem help you solve another problem? Which of these problems are related to each other?

As students explain their strategies, listen for examples where students are finding general rules to help them solve related problems. For example, when solving 10 x 7, one student commented, "You take half of it, so you get 5 x 7, which I know is 35, and then you double 35."

Many students will see a pattern when a number is multiplied by 10. They may notice may be that you always add a zero and be unable to explain why. The **Teacher Note**, Multiplying by Multiples of 10 (p. 66), provides some ideas for discussing this pattern with students.

Encourage students to talk about how they solved the final problem in the cluster, 25 × 7. There will probably be a variety of strategies, including pulling apart the problem into more manageable parts (10 × 7, 10 × 7, 5 × 7), skip counting by 25's, or thinking in terms of other key relationships (there are four 25's in 100). All of these ways are acceptable approaches.

Making Up a Cluster Problem   On the board or overhead, put up the problem 21 × 8 and ask students to make up a set of cluster problems that would help them to solve the problem. Encourage them to think about how they might break apart this larger problem into smaller, more familiar problems.

List their ideas on the board. There will probably be more than one cluster of problems for this multiplication problem. If there is time, or for homework, have students solve the cluster problems they created.

Activity

Class Discussion: How Many Boxes Do You Need?

In this discussion, students discuss the solution to one of the division word problems they have been working on (Problem 2, Student Sheet 9). Put the following problem on the board or overhead:

Students have collected 90 cans for a recycling project. How many boxes do they need to store the cans? Each box holds 12 cans.

Have students demonstrate their strategies for solving this problem. Some students may need cubes, others may want to record their strategy on the overhead or board. In all cases, make sure students represent the problem using division notation in addition to explaining how they solved the problem.

Sessions 2, 3, and 4 Follow-Up

At the end of Session 3, assign students multiplication clusters, Sets K and L, Student Sheet 7, page 7 of 7. If students did not finish making up and solving a set of cluster problems in class, you may suggest they do so for homework.

Homework

One of the mathematical "tricks" we all learned to help us with hard multiplication was the rule, "When you multiply by 10, just add a zero; when you multiply by 100, add two zeroes; and so on." Even if you don't teach this rule explicitly, students readily see the pattern of adding zeroes as they work on related multiplication problems, such as 2 × 7 and 20 × 7, and will invent the rule themselves. While this pattern is a very useful one, the mathematics behind it is fairly difficult for students at this age to grasp completely. If rules are simply memorized and used without thought, they are often misremembered or misapplied as problems become more complex.

Therefore, while we want to encourage students to use the patterns they've discovered, we also want them to double-check their work using other strategies and to be able to estimate that their solution is a reasonable one. For example, if a student solves 5 × 30 by saying "It's like 5 times 3 and add a zero, so it's 150," we would ask, "And how do you know 150 is a reasonable answer? Is there another way you can prove it? How do you know it's not 1500?"

By using arrays, students have a chance to see how multiplying by 10 and multiples of 10 works. Imagine the array for 8 × 1. There is one 8 in this array, or you can think of it as eight 1's. Similarly, imagine the array for 8 × 10.

Looking at it one way, there are ten 8's; looking at it another way, there are eight 10's. For 8 × 100, there are one hundred 8's or eight 100's. Our number system is based on units based on powers of ten: ones, tens, hundreds, thousands, and so forth. Each time we multiply a number by one of these units, we get a multiple of that unit:

8 × 1 =	8 ones =	8
8 × 10 =	8 tens =	80
8 × 100 =	8 hundreds =	800
8 × 1000 =	8 thousands =	8000

It may look like we are just "adding zeroes." In fact, we are generating the same number of groups of larger and larger units: 8 ones, 8 tens, 8 hundreds, 8 thousands.

Multiplying by multiples of 10, 100, and 1000—for example, 4 × 20 or 8 × 30, 6 × 700, 2 × 6000—is a bit more complex, but is based on multiplication by 10, 100, and so on. When students imagine an array for 8 × 30 and relate it to the array for 8 × 10, they begin to see that they are multiplying *8 groups of three 10's* or 8 × (3 × 10). By visualizing and discussing what the arrays for such multiplication problems look like, they can begin to develop a sound basis for understanding the "add the zero" rule.

Problems That Look Hard But Aren't

What Happens

In the final session of this unit, students work in small groups to generate a list of "hard" multiplication pairs (or relationships). The class compiles a list of these pairs and discusses which are the most difficult relationships to learn and which they have developed strategies for solving. They solve a two-digit multiplication problem as a whole class. As an assessment activity, students solve another two-digit problem in two different ways. Their work focuses on:

- applying multiplication relationships to a two-digit problem
- using what they know about multiplication to discuss and solve harder problems

Materials

- Interlocking cubes
- One-centimeter graph paper (1–2 per student)
- Student Sheet 10 (1 per student)

Discussing Multiplication Pairs

Organize students into groups of four. Each group is responsible for making a list of the five multiplication pairs that are the most difficult to learn (up to 12's table). You might suggest to students that they look back to the list they made when they played Multiplication Pairs. The group needs to agree on five pairs to present to the class. Groups will need 5 to 10 minutes to prepare their lists.

Which Pairs Are Hard for You?

Each group presents the list of multiplication pairs that its members consider the most difficult to learn. There may be pairs that are common to many groups' lists. As you record these pairs on the board, put a check mark next to any that are repeated (instead of recording them more than once). From this list determine a class list of the five to eight multiplication relationships that are the most difficult to learn. These will be the ones that have the most check marks next to them.

There may be some difference of opinion about pairs some students consider hard and others do not. Have students share strategies for how they learned or remember these relationships. Some strategies students have used in the past for learning hard relationships are breaking the problem into two easier problems, relating the problem to one they already know, or picking one or two hard problems each day to learn. The **Dialogue Box**, Strategies for Learning "Hard Problems," p. 71 gives some examples of student strategies.

Problems That Look Hard But Really Aren't

Present a two-digit by one-digit multiplication problem such as this on the board or overhead:

$$31 \times 6$$

Some people think this looks like a hard multiplication problem. During the past two weeks you've been developing strategies for solving these kinds of problems. I'd like you to talk briefly with the person next to you about how you would solve this problem.

Students talk with the people near them about how they would solve the problem. Bring the group together to share strategies for approaching this multiplication problem. Record students' ideas on the board. Ask students why some people might think this was a hard multiplication problem.

What are some other two-digit multiplication problems that look hard but really aren't?

Record this list on the board and save it. Students will choose one problem from the list to do for homework.

Assessment

Solving Two-Digit Multiplication Problems

Students work alone to solve the next problem. They solve the problem in two different ways and write about how they solved the problem. Graph paper and interlocking cubes should be available for those students who need them.

Pass out a copy of Student Sheet 10, Two Ways to Solve a Problem (p. 96), to each student. Tell students you would like to get an idea of how they are thinking about multiplication problems they have been doing and what kinds of strategies they are using.

These responses are one way of assessing a student's understanding of multiplication problems. See **Teacher Note**, Two Ways to Solve 27 × 4 (p. 70). As you look at student papers, there are several questions you can focus on:

- Are students keeping track of their work carefully?
- Are students becoming fluent in the basic multiplication relationships?
- Do students demonstrate an understanding of partitioning large numbers into more familiar parts as a way of multiplying?
- Are students using tools (centimeter paper, cubes) appropriately to help them solve the problem?

Choosing Student Work to Save

As the unit ends, you may want to use one of the following options for creating a record of students' work on this unit:

■ Students look back through their folders or notebooks and write about what they learned in this unit, what they remember most, and what was hard or easy for them. Students could do this during their writing time.

■ Students select one or two pieces of their work as their best, and you also choose one or two pieces of their work to be saved. This work is saved in a portfolio for the year. You might include students' written solutions to the assessment, Creating and Solving Division Problems (Investigation 2, Sessions 7 and 8), and any other assessment tasks from this unit. Students can create a separate page with brief comments describing the pieces of work.

■ You may want to send a selection of work home for parents to see. Students write a cover letter describing their work in this unit. This work should be returned if you are keeping a year-long portfolio of mathematics work for each student.

Session 5 Follow-Up

🏠 **Homework**

Students learn the five to eight multiplication pairs that the class agreed were the most difficult to learn. They choose one multiplication problem from their group's list of "Problems That Look Hard But Aren't." They should solve this problem and then write about: "Why This Problem Looks Hard But Is Not."

Most likely, all students will not have had the opportunity to finish every choice item. You might decide to have these choices remain in the classroom for students to work on during their free time or for homework.

Note: Students will need to use their sets of arrays later in the year in the unit *Packages and Groups*. We suggest students keep their bags of arrays in their current math folders and continue to use them as a way of learning the basic multiplication relationships. You will need to save array transparencies.

As you look at students' work for this assessment, consider whether each student has developed reliable strategies and can record clearly the steps used to solve the problem. Has the student used a combination of addition and multiplication strategies? Can the student pull apart a "hard" multiplication problem into smaller related multiplication problems? Asking students to solve problems in more than one way helps them to think flexibly and also gives them a way to check their work. The following are examples of students' solutions to the problem 27 × 4.

■ *Addition Strategies.* Many students see this problem as one of repeated addition.

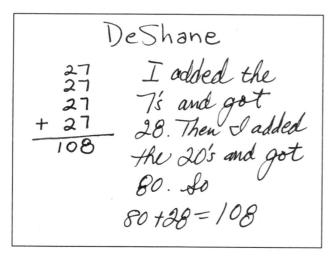

Some students used the same notation but explained that they "skip counted by 27's."

Teresa

$$27$$
$$27$$
$$27$$
$$+ \ 27$$
$$108$$

I skip counted by 27s

Still others may know that if two 27's is equal to 54 then four 27's is double that. One student represented the problem in this way:

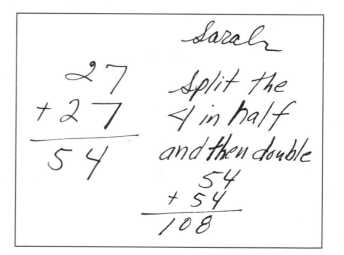

Similarly, another student wrote,

Sarah

$$27$$
$$+ \ 27$$
$$54$$

Split the 4 in half and then double

$$54$$
$$+ \ 54$$
$$108$$

Continued on next page

■ *Multiplication Strategies.* We expect that many students will be able to break apart the problem into smaller, more familiar multiplication problems as one of their strategies. Here is how one student kept track of each part of the problem and of the totals of those problems:

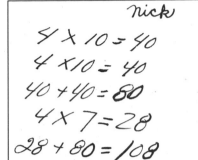

Some students will break 27 into 20 + 7, multiply each by 4, and add the subtotals:

> "I counted 20 four times and got 80. Then I said 7 × 4 and got 28, and then I added them together and got 108."

Here is another version of a student's record of this solution:

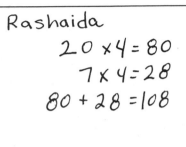

D I A L O G U E   B O X

Strategies for Learning "Hard Problems"

This discussion occurred while students were working on the activity Which Pairs Are Hard for You (p. 67).

DeShane: I think 6 × 8 is a hard problem. It's on my list every time.

[Lots of students groan and agree with DeShane. A few students in the class disagree.]

Teresa: I had 6 × 8 on my list too, but you can think of it like 6 × 4 and 6 × 4. That's 24 plus 24, and that's easier to figure out for me. It's like the Small Array/Big Array game. 6 × 4 is the small array and 6 × 8 is the big array, so it's a match.

Rashaida: I just think of 5 × 8 which I know is equal to 40, then I add 8 more.

DeShane: That's hard.

Qi Sun: I just memorized it. I kept thinking, 6 × 8 is equal to 48, 6 × 8 is equal to 48; then I just remembered it.

Those are some interesting strategies for remembering a hard problem. Teresa broke the problem down into pieces she knew. Rashaida connected it to a fact she already knew and then added on, and Qi Sun practiced it over and over again. Any other ideas? How about skip counting?,

Sarah: You could skip count by 8's, but that's tricky.

DeShane: Or you could do 6's, that's tricky too. I think I'll try skip counting by 6's with my partner today at Choice Time.

Sounds like a good idea.

Counting Around the Class

Basic Activity

Students count around the class by a particular number. That is, if counting by 2's, the first student says "2," the next student says "4," the next "6," and so forth. Before the count starts, students try to predict on what number the count will end. During and after the count, students discuss relationships between the chosen factor and its multiples.

Counting Around the Class is designed to give students practice with counting by many different numbers and to foster numerical reasoning about the relationships among factors and their multiples. Students focus on:

- becoming familiar with multiplication patterns
- relating factors to their multiples
- developing number sense about multiplication and division relationships

Materials

- Calculators (for variation)

Procedure

Step 1. Choose a number to count by. For example, if the class has been working with quarters recently, you might want to count by 25's.

Step 2. Ask students to predict the target number. "If we count by 25's around the class, what number will we end up on?" Encourage students to talk about how they could figure this out without doing the actual counting.

Step 3. Count around the class by your chosen number. "25 . . . 50 . . . 75 . . ." If some students seem uncertain about what comes next, you might put the numbers on the board as they count; seeing the visual patterns can help some students with the spoken one.

You might count around a second time by the same number, starting with a different person, so that students will hear the pattern more than once and have their turns at different points in the sequence.

Step 4. Pause in the middle of the count to look back. "We're up to 375 counting by 25's. How many students have we counted so far? How do you know?"

Step 5. Extend the problem. Ask questions like these: "Which of your predictions were reasonable? Which were possible? Which were impossible?" (A student might remark, for example, "You couldn't have 510 for 25's because 25 only lands on the 25's, the 50's, the 75's, and the 100's.")

"What if we had 32 students in this class instead of 28? Then where would we end up?"

"What if we used a different number? This time we counted by 25's and ended on 700; what if we counted by 50's? What number do you think we would end on? Why do you think it will be twice as big? How did you figure that out?"

Variations

Multiplication Practice Use single-digit numbers to provide practice with multiplication (that is, count by 2's, 3's, 4's, 5's, 7's, and so forth). In counting by numbers other than 1, students usually first become comfortable with 2's, 5's, and 10's, which have very regular patterns. Soon they can begin to count by more difficult single-digit numbers: 3, 4, 6, and (later) 7, 8, and 9.

Landmark Numbers When students are learning about money or about our base ten system of numeration, they can count by 20's, 25's, 50's, 100's, and 1000's. Counting by multiples of 10 and 100 (30's, 40's, 600's) will support students' growing familiarity with the base 10 system of numeration.

Continued on next page

Making Connections When you choose harder numbers, pick those that are related in some way to numbers students are very familiar with. For example, once students are comfortable counting by 25's, have them count by 75's. Ask students how knowing the 25's will help them count by 75's. If students are fluent with 3's, try counting by 6's or by 30's. If students are fluent with 10's and 20's, start working on 15's. If they are comfortable counting by 15's, ask them to count by 150's or 1500's.

Large Numbers Introduce large numbers, such as 2000, 5000, 1500, or 10,000, so that students begin to work with combinations of these less familiar numbers.

Using the Calculator On some days you might have everyone use a calculator, or have a few students use the calculators to skip count while you are counting around the class. On most calculators, the equals (=) key provides a built-in constant function, allowing you to skip count easily. For example, if you want to skip count by 25's, you press your starting number (let's say 0), the operation you want to use (in this case, +), and the number you want to count by (in this case, 25). Then, press the equals key each time you want to add 25. So, if you press

| 0 | + | 25 | = | = | = | = |

you will see on your screen 25, 50, 75, 100.

Special Notes

Letting Students Prepare When introducing an unfamiliar number to count with, students may need some preparation before they try to count around the class. Ask students to work in pairs to figure out, with whatever materials they want to use, what number the count will end on.

Avoiding Competition It is important to be sensitive to potential embarrassment or competition if some students have difficulty figuring out their number. One teacher allowed students to volunteer for the next number, rather than counting in a particular order. Other teachers have made the count a cooperative effort, establishing an atmosphere in which students readily helped each other, and anyone felt free to ask for help.

Related Homework Options

Counting Patterns Students write out a counting pattern up to a target number (for example, by 25's up to 500). Then they write about what patterns they see in their counting. Calculators can be used for this.

Mystery Number Problems Provide an ending number and ask students to figure out what factor they would have to count by to reach it. For example: "I'm thinking of a mystery number. I figured out that if we counted around the class by my mystery number today, we would get to 2800. What is the mystery number?"

Or, you might provide students with the final number and the factor, and ask them to figure out the number of students in the class. "When a certain class counts by 25's, the last student says 550. How many students are in the class?" Calculators can be used.

Multiple BINGO

Basic Activity

This game can be played either as a whole class or with a partner or a small group. Students can play it independently, but it's more fun to play with other people. The object of the game is to color five numbers in a row, either across, up and down, or diagonally. The factor cards tell you what numbers you can color in. The number you color in must be a multiple of the factor card.

Multiple BINGO is designed to give students practice with finding multiples of numbers. Either by skip counting or using multiplication pairs, this activity fosters numerical reasoning about the relationships among factors and their multiples. Students focus on:

- relating factors to their multiples
- becoming familiar with multiplication patterns
- developing number sense about multiplication and division relationships.

Materials

- 100 chart (one for each player)
- Deck of factor cards (one deck per 2–3 students)
- Crayons or markers
- Optional: students may use 100 charts on which they have highlighted 2's, 3's, 4's, 5's, and so on; or they may use calculators

Procedure

Playing in a small group

Step 1. Gather materials. Each player has a 100 chart and a marker. Put the factor cards in a pile in the middle of the table. Players take turns picking a factor card for the group.

Step 2. Choose a multiple. Every player colors in *one* number that is a multiple of the factor card and writes the factor in the square. For example, if someone turns over a 5 card, any one of the numbers 5, 10, 15, 20, 25, and so on, can be chosen. The next player picks a factor card and again every player chooses *one* number to color in.

Step 3. Using a *Wild Card*. If a *Wild Card* is picked, the player who picked it can decide on the factor to be used. Any number from 1 to 100 can be chosen when a *Wild Card* is drawn. For game strategy, the player should choose a number that helps his or her game but doesn't help the other players. Often the most useful number to pick is a prime number, such as 23, to fill in a gap between other multiples; other players could mark 23, or 46, or 69, or 92.

Step 4. Color five multiples in a row. The game continues until a player colors five numbers in a row and gets BINGO. Players can choose to continue until other players also get five in a row.

Variations

Whole Class Game   This game can be played as a whole class. A leader, the teacher or a student, draws the factor cards for the whole class. If a *Wild Card* is drawn, the leader calls on a player to choose a factor for the group to use. The object of the game is to cover five numbers in a row. You might want to continue play until every player has covered five in a row. When the class plays as a large group, there is the option for students who are new to the game to collaborate with another student.

Limiting the Factors   An easier version of Multiple BINGO is to use only the 2's, 3's, 4's, and 5's factor cards and a few *Wild Cards*. Students can use the 100 charts they have highlighted for the multiples of 2, 3, 4, and 5 as references while they play the game. As students highlight 100 charts for new multiples, add those new factor cards to the game.

Continued on next page

Limiting the 100 Chart When students first play Multiple BINGO, they will tend to use only "easy" numbers—especially the single-digit numbers and the multiples of 10. To encourage them to use more difficult numbers, you might:

1. Have them omit the top row and right column of the 100 chart.

2. Insist they start with a number near the middle of the chart.

3. Give two points for a win that is a diagonal (five numbers next to each other on any diagonal is fine). This may encourage them to notice the 9's and 11's tables on the two main diagonals.

Other Ways to Win Once students are familiar with the basic game, vary the ways to win. For example, a "win" could be defined as coloring six multiples in a row or coloring in a 2 × 3 rectangle of multiples.

Special Notes

Using Resources Encourage students to use calculators or their sets of highlighted 100 charts they made for the multiples 2 to 12 as a way of determining multiples for the factor cards.

Reusing the 100 Chart Students can use a contrasting color to play another game on the same 100 chart. Some teachers have laminated a set of 100 charts that can be wiped off after each game. Students will need to use either a crayon or an overhead marker with these laminated charts.

Related Homework Options

Playing Multiple BINGO at Home. Students can play Multiple BINGO at home. They will need 100 charts and a set of factor cards.

The following activities will help ensure that this unit is comprehensible to students who are acquiring English as a second language. The suggested approach is based on *The Natural Approach: Language Acquisition in the Classroom* by Stephen D. Krashen and Tracy D. Terrell (Alemany Press, 1983). The intent is for second-language learners to acquire new vocabulary in an active, meaningful context.

Note that *acquiring* a word is different from *learning* a word. Depending on their level of proficiency, students may be able to comprehend a word upon hearing it during an investigation without being able to say it. Other students may be able to use the word orally, but not read or write it. The goal is to help students naturally acquire targeted vocabulary at their present level of proficiency.

We suggest using these activities just before the related investigations. The activities can also be led by English-proficient students.

Investigations 1–3

packaged

1. Display a carton of eggs, a bag of pretzels, and a box of pencils.

2. Explain that *packaging* something means to put items together.

3. Point out how the displayed items are packaged differently.

   The eggs are packaged in a cardboard carton. The pretzels are packaged in a bag. The pencils are packaged inside a box.

4. Point out how some items are arranged in rows and others are not.

5. Ask students to decide other ways eggs, pretzels, and pencils could or could not be packaged.

   Would you package eggs inside a plastic bag? Could you package pretzels inside a box? Why? Why not?

related

1. Show students three clear plastic bags with the following items placed inside:

   Bag 1: drawing materials such as: oil pastels, marker pens, and crayons;

   Bag 2: items of all one color

   Bag 3: paper clips, rubber bands, string

2. Identify the items in Bag 1. Explain that although each item in the bag is different, they are actually all related to each other. Further explain that this means there is something the same about all three items. Ask yes or no questions to help students identify the relationship of these items.

   Are the items related to each other because they are all the same size? Are the items related to each other because they are all made out of the same material? Are the items related to each other because they are all the same color? Are the items related to each other because they are all used for drawing?

3. Continue with the same format for Bags 2 and 3.

4. Challenge students' comprehension of the word *related* by playing the following game. Have students collect various items from home and around the classroom.

   Tell them to put three related items into a plastic bag. Then have them put in one more item that is not related to the other items. Have students share their bags. Challenge the other students in the group to identify which item in each bag is not related and why.

strategy, strategies

1. Display 12 interlocking cubes in front of the students.

2. Ask them to think of a fast way to count the number of cubes in this group.

3. Point out that there are several different ways to do this task as you show examples of different strategies. Be sure to articulate your actions as you are doing them. Emphasize that there is not just one "correct" strategy.

   One strategy might be to divide the cubes in half, count one of these groups, and then double that number. Another strategy or idea might be to count the cubes by 2's, 3's, or 4's.

4. Next, pair students and have them sit around a large pile of interlocking cubes. Challenge them to think of a strategy for using the cubes to make three towers as quickly as possible. Tell them each tower needs to have six cubes.

5. When students have completed the task, ask questions about their individual strategies.

   Did you both work on building each tower? Did that strategy help you finish quickly? Did one person count and another build? Did that strategy help you finish quickly? Did you count by 2's? Did that strategy help you finish quickly?

Blackline Masters

for *Arrays and Shares*

Dear Family,

In mathematics, our class is starting a new unit called *Arrays and Shares*. This unit focuses on multiplication and division. Students begin the unit by looking at things that are arranged in rows, for example, juice packs, egg cartons, and rows of chairs. Through examining these rectangular arrangements (or arrays), they begin to visualize important aspects of multiplication, for example, that the solution to 7 × 6 is the same as the solution to 6 × 7.

As students go on to work on two-digit multiplication and related division problems, it is critical that they visualize how to pull apart the numbers they are working with. To solve these harder problems, students learn to use related problems they already know how to solve. For example, the problem 7 × 23 can be solved by breaking the problem into more familiar parts: 7 × 10, 7 × 10, and 7 × 3.

While our class is studying multiplication and division you can help in the following ways:

Look for items around your house or at the grocery store that are packaged or arranged in rectangular arrays. Tiles on the floor, egg cartons, window panes, and six-packs of juice cans are examples of rectangular arrays. Talk with your child about the dimensions (rows and columns) and discuss ways to figure out the total number.

Play the Array Games that your child brings home for homework.

Help your child practice skip counting by 3's, 4's, 5's, and so forth.

When your child brings home problems, encourage your child to explain his or her strategies to you. Ask questions, such as, "How did you figure that out?" and "Tell me your thinking about this problem," but don't provide answers or methods. Show that you are interested in how your child is thinking and reasoning about these problems.

Please don't teach your child step-by-step procedures for computing multiplication and division. Too often we find that children at this age memorize the multiplication and division procedures but cannot recognize situations in which multiplication and division are useful. We will gradually support students this year in developing several strategies for carrying out multiplication and division problems, but we would prefer they not memorize procedures at this time.

Thank you for your interest in your child's study of mathematics. We are looking forward to an exciting few weeks of work on multiplication and division.

Sincerely,

Multiplication Clusters

Solve each cluster of multiplication problems.
Look for ways the problems in each cluster
are related.

$2 \times 4 =$ $4 \times 4 =$ $\begin{array}{r} 8 \\ \times\ 4 \\ \hline \end{array}$ $\begin{array}{r} 12 \\ \times\ 4 \\ \hline \end{array}$

$7 \times 2 =$ $\begin{array}{r} 8 \\ \times\ 2 \\ \hline \end{array}$ $9 \times 2 =$

$5 \times 6 =$ $6 \times 6 =$ $\begin{array}{r} 7 \\ \times\ 6 \\ \hline \end{array}$

$3 \times 5 =$ $\begin{array}{r} 6 \\ \times\ 5 \\ \hline \end{array}$ $\begin{array}{r} 12 \\ \times\ 5 \\ \hline \end{array}$

$\begin{array}{r} 9 \\ \times\ 3 \\ \hline \end{array}$ $\begin{array}{r} 9 \\ \times\ 6 \\ \hline \end{array}$ $9 \times 12 =$

More Multiplication Clusters

Solve each cluster of multiplication problems.
Look for ways the problems in each cluster
are related.

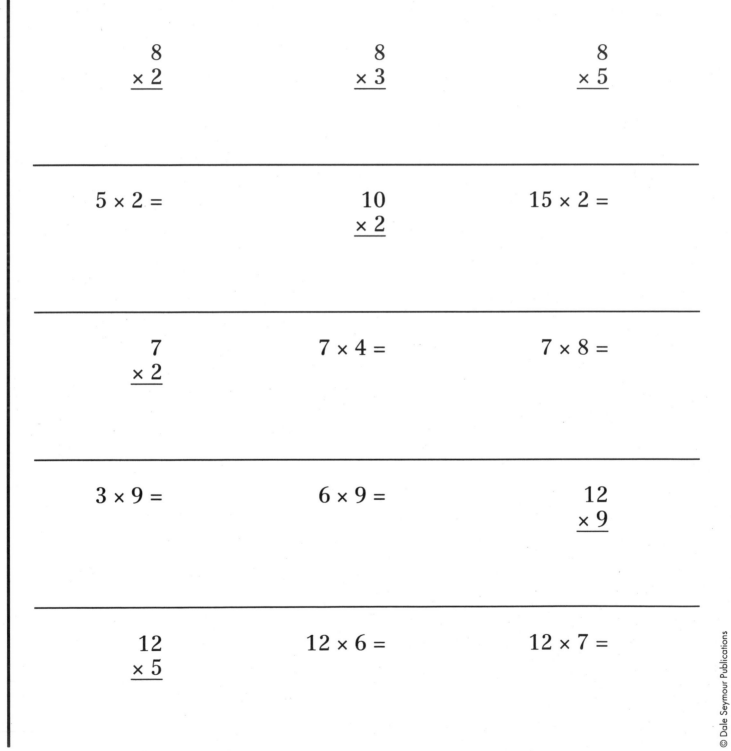

$$\begin{array}{r} 8 \\ \times\ 2 \\ \hline \end{array} \qquad \begin{array}{r} 8 \\ \times\ 3 \\ \hline \end{array} \qquad \begin{array}{r} 8 \\ \times\ 5 \\ \hline \end{array}$$

$5 \times 2 =$ $\qquad$ $\begin{array}{r} 10 \\ \times\ 2 \\ \hline \end{array}$ $\qquad$ $15 \times 2 =$

$\begin{array}{r} 7 \\ \times\ 2 \\ \hline \end{array}$ $\qquad$ $7 \times 4 =$ $\qquad$ $7 \times 8 =$

$3 \times 9 =$ $\qquad$ $6 \times 9 =$ $\qquad$ $\begin{array}{r} 12 \\ \times\ 9 \\ \hline \end{array}$

$\begin{array}{r} 12 \\ \times\ 5 \\ \hline \end{array}$ $\qquad$ $12 \times 6 =$ $\qquad$ $12 \times 7 =$

Things That Come in Arrays

Item	Total	Dimensions	Draw the Array

What Do You Do with the Extras?

1. There are 36 people who are taking a trip in some small vans. Each van holds 8 people. How many vans will they need?

2. Eight people are going to share 36 crackers equally. How many crackers will each person get?

3. Eight people are going to share 36 balloons equally. How many balloons will each person get?

4. There are 36 students who are going to see a movie. Each row holds 8 people. How many rows will they fill up?

5. Eight friends raised 36 dollars by washing people's cars. They want to share the money equally. How much should each person get?

What's the Story?

Write a story for each division problem.
Then solve the problem.

1. $42 \div 7$

2. $8 \overline{)52}$

3. $9 \overline{)63}$

4. $49 \div 4$

Word Problems

Solve each word problem. Write your solution in words.
Then, use division notation to write an equation
that represents the problem.

1. Juice comes in 6-packs. How many 6-packs would
    we need to buy if we bought a can of juice for
    everyone in our class?

2. There are 46 people attending a concert. The chairs
    are set up in rows of 7. How many rows will be
    filled?

3. The book you are reading has 17 chapters. If you
    read 2 chapters in 3 hours, how many hours will it
    take you to read the book?

4. There will be 9 people at my pizza party. If each
    person eats 3 slices of pizza and each pizza has 8
    slices, how many pizzas should I order?

Multiplication Clusters (page 1 of 7)

Materials: Multiplication Clusters—Sets A–L

With a partner, choose a multiplication cluster set to discuss. You may work on the problems in the cluster set in any order. You and your partner should talk about:

- How would you solve each problem in the set?
- Does knowing the answer to one problem help you solve another problem?
- How are these problems related to each other?

Discuss two or three cluster sets with your partner.

Write about one of the cluster sets. Write the answers to the problems and also write about how you did the problems. You and your partner can choose to write about the same cluster set or different sets.

Read each other's writing about the cluster problems. If something isn't clear, explain to your partner what you don't understand. Offer a suggestion about what they could add to make their writing clearer.

Multiplication Clusters (page 2 of 7)

SETS A & B

After you solve each cluster, write about how you solved it.

Tell how you used an answer to one problem to help you find the answer to another problem.

SET A

$3 \times 4 =$

$3 \times 10 =$

$10 \times 4 =$

$3 \times 40 =$

$4 \times 30 =$

SET B

$5 \times 3 =$

$5 \times 10 =$

$10 \times 3 =$

$30 \times 5 =$

$50 \times 3 =$

Multiplication Clusters (page 3 of 7)

SETS C & D

After you solve each cluster, write about how you solved it.

Tell how you used an answer to one problem to help you find the answer to another problem.

SET C

$2 \times 5 =$

$3 \times 5 =$

$10 \times 5 =$

$30 \times 5 =$

$32 \times 5 =$

SET D

$5 \times 7 =$

$10 \times 7 =$

$2 \times 7 =$

$20 \times 7 =$

$25 \times 7 =$

Multiplication Clusters (page 4 of 7)

SETS E & F

After you solve each cluster, write about how you solved it.

Tell how you used an answer to one problem to help you find the answer to another problem.

SET E

$3 \times 5 =$

$10 \times 5 =$

$20 \times 5 =$

$23 \times 5 =$

SET F

$3 \times 6 =$

$3 \times 10 =$

$6 \times 10 =$

$3 \times 60 =$

$60 \times 3 =$

Multiplication Clusters (page 5 of 7)

SETS G & H

After you solve each cluster, write about how you solved it.

Tell how you used an answer to one problem to help you find the answer to another problem.

SET G

$2 \times 5 =$

$2 \times 10 =$

$10 \times 5 =$

$2 \times 50 =$

SET H

$7 \times 2 =$

$7 \times 10 =$

$2 \times 10 =$

$7 \times 20 =$

$2 \times 70 =$

Multiplication Clusters (page 6 of 7)

SETS I & J

After you solve each cluster, write about how you solved it.

Tell how you used an answer to one problem to help you find the answer to another problem.

SET I

$5 \times 3 =$

$10 \times 6 =$

$6 \times 5 =$

$60 \times 5 =$

$6 \times 50 =$

SET J

$8 \times 2 =$

$8 \times 10 =$

$20 \times 8 =$

$10 \times 2 =$

$80 \times 2 =$

Multiplication Clusters (page 7 of 7)

SETS K & L

After you solve each cluster, write about how you solved it.

Tell how you used an answer to one problem to help you find the answer to another problem.

SET K

$10 \times 6 =$

$3 \times 6 =$

$13 \times 6 =$

SET L

$4 \times 6 =$

$4 \times 3 =$

$4 \times 30 =$

$4 \times 36 =$

Problems About Our Class

Solve each word problem. Use division notation to
write an equation that represents the problem.
Write how you solved the problem or draw a picture.

1. Suppose we want to arrange our desks into smaller
    groups of students. How many groups would we
    have if there were 5 desks in a group?

    How many groups would we have if there were 4
    desks in a group?

2. There are 65 students going on a field trip. We
    need adult chaperones and vans. For every
    10 students, we need one adult. Each van holds
    9 people. How many adults do we need?
    How many vans do we need?

3. The field trip policy at our school is that there must
    be one adult for every 10 students. How many
    adults would our class need to take on a field trip?

    How many adults would we need if 4 classes like
    ours went on a field trip?

Recycling Problems

Solve each word problem. Use division notation to
write an equation that represents the problem.
Write how you solved the problem or draw a picture.

1. Some fourth graders collected cans to recycle.
    They have a total of 46 cans. They need to store
    them in boxes that hold 12 cans. How many boxes
    do they need?

2. On the first day of class-wide collections, students
    collected 90 cans. How many boxes did they need
    to store the cans? Each box held 12 cans.

3. The next day they collected 45 more cans. How
    many cans did they collect during the first two
    days? How many boxes did they use for storage?

Two Ways to Solve a Problem

Solve this problem in two different ways:

$$27 \times 4$$

After each way, write about how you did it. Be sure to include:

- ▪ what materials you used to solve this problem, if any
- ▪ how you solved it, and
- ▪ an explanation of your thinking as you solved it.

First Way:

Second Way:

100 Chart

1	2	3	4	5	6	7	8	9	10
11	12	13	14	15	16	17	18	19	20
21	22	23	24	25	26	27	28	29	30
31	32	33	34	35	36	37	38	39	40
41	42	43	44	45	46	47	48	49	50
51	52	53	54	55	56	57	58	59	60
61	62	63	64	65	66	67	68	69	70
71	72	73	74	75	76	77	78	79	80
81	82	83	84	85	86	87	88	89	90
91	92	93	94	95	96	97	98	99	100

100 Chart (4 to a page)

1	2	3	4	5	6	7	8	9	10
11	12	13	14	15	16	17	18	19	20
21	22	23	24	25	26	27	28	29	30
31	32	33	34	35	36	37	38	39	40
41	42	43	44	45	46	47	48	49	50
51	52	53	54	55	56	57	58	59	60
61	62	63	64	65	66	67	68	69	70
71	72	73	74	75	76	77	78	79	80
81	82	83	84	85	86	87	88	89	90
91	92	93	94	95	96	97	98	99	100

1	2	3	4	5	6	7	8	9	10
11	12	13	14	15	16	17	18	19	20
21	22	23	24	25	26	27	28	29	30
31	32	33	34	35	36	37	38	39	40
41	42	43	44	45	46	47	48	49	50
51	52	53	54	55	56	57	58	59	60
61	62	63	64	65	66	67	68	69	70
71	72	73	74	75	76	77	78	79	80
81	82	83	84	85	86	87	88	89	90
91	92	93	94	95	96	97	98	99	100

1	2	3	4	5	6	7	8	9	10
11	12	13	14	15	16	17	18	19	20
21	22	23	24	25	26	27	28	29	30
31	32	33	34	35	36	37	38	39	40
41	42	43	44	45	46	47	48	49	50
51	52	53	54	55	56	57	58	59	60
61	62	63	64	65	66	67	68	69	70
71	72	73	74	75	76	77	78	79	80
81	82	83	84	85	86	87	88	89	90
91	92	93	94	95	96	97	98	99	100

1	2	3	4	5	6	7	8	9	10
11	12	13	14	15	16	17	18	19	20
21	22	23	24	25	26	27	28	29	30
31	32	33	34	35	36	37	38	39	40
41	42	43	44	45	46	47	48	49	50
51	52	53	54	55	56	57	58	59	60
61	62	63	64	65	66	67	68	69	70
71	72	73	74	75	76	77	78	79	80
81	82	83	84	85	86	87	88	89	90
91	92	93	94	95	96	97	98	99	100

How to Make Array Cards

What You Will Need

- ■ Copies of Array Card Sheets
- ■ A plastic bag to keep the cards in
- ■ Scissors, pencil

What to Do

1. Carefully cut out each array on the Array Card sheets. Follow the outlines of each array as exactly as you can.

2. Each card has two sides. On the array side of the card, write the **dimensions** of the array. Example:

3. On the other side (the blank side), write the total number of squares in the array. Example:

$$24$$

Also write one of the dimensions of the array, very lightly, along one side. Use pencil so you can erase later.

4. Write your initials on each card. Put them in the plastic bag. Keep your cards together at all times!

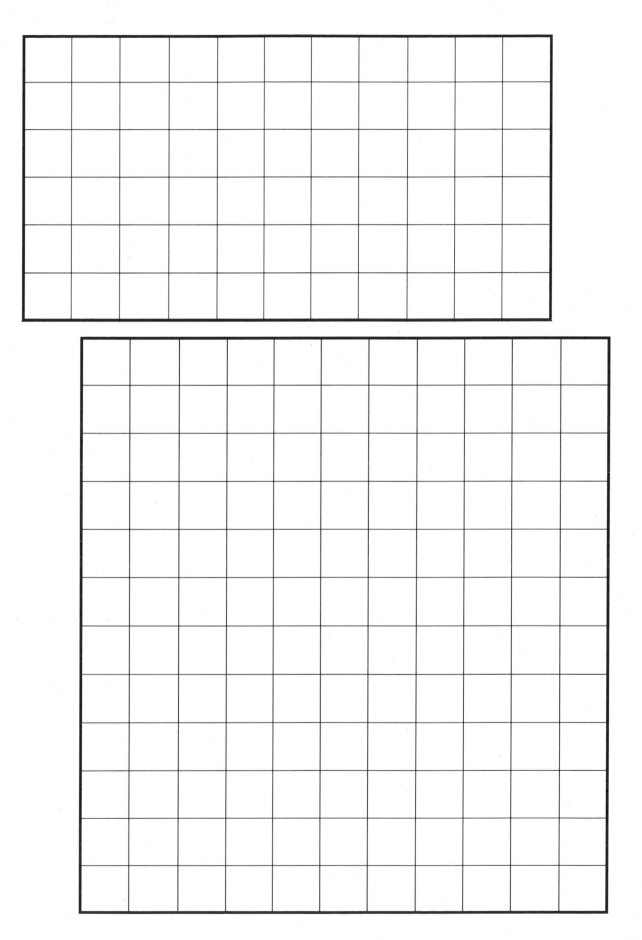

How to Play Multiplication Pairs

Materials

- Set of array cards
- Paper and pencil

Players: 1, 2, or 3

How to Play

1. Spread out all the array cards in front of you. Some should be turned up, showing the dimensions. Others should be turned over to show the total.

2. Choose an array card and put your finger on it. (Don't pick it up until you say the answer.) If the dimensions are showing, you must give the total. If the total is showing, you must say the dimensions of the grid. The shape of the array will help you!

   For example: Suppose you pick an array with total 36 showing. The dimensions could be 6×6, or 9×4, or 12×3. You must decide which is right. The shape of the array is a good clue.

3. Turn the card over to check your answer. If your answer is correct, then pick up the card.

4. If you are playing with a partner, take turns choosing and identifying cards. Play until you have picked up all the cards.

   While you are playing, make lists for yourself of "pairs that I know" and "pairs that I don't know yet." Keep these lists in your math folder.

How to Play Count and Compare

Materials: Set of array cards

Players: 2 or 3

How to Play

1. If you are playing with a partner, sit across from each other. If three people are playing, sit in a circle.

2. Deal out the array cards with the total sides face down. Players should all have the same number of cards. Set aside any that are left over.

3. Place your cards in a stack in front of you, with the total side face down.

4. Players take the top card from their stacks and place these cards side by side (total sides still face down).

5. Decide which array is largest. You can do this just by looking, or by skip counting by rows to find the total of each. Counting the squares by 1's is not allowed.

6. The player with the largest array takes the cards, after proving that it is the largest.

7. Sometimes arrays of the same size may be played in one turn—like this:

When this happens, the players decide together who will get the cards. Once a rule is decided, it cannot be changed until the game is over.

8. The game is over when time is up or one player runs out of cards.

How to Play Small Array/Big Array

Materials: Set of array cards

Players: 2

How to Play

1. Deal out 10 array cards to each player with the dimensions side up. Spread out the cards in front of you.

2. Spread out 6 more cards, dimensions side up, in the center of the table. Place the remaining cards in a deck in the center of the table.

3. The goal is to make a "match" by covering a big array with two or three smaller arrays. Players take turns.

4. From your smaller arrays, choose one that matches one dimension of a big array in the center of the table.

5. If none of your array cards matches, you can choose a card that matches a dimension of the big array from the center of the table. Or you can pick the top card from the deck and play it if you can.

6. If you use an array from the center of the table to cover another array, you can either replace it with a card from the deck, or discard one of your array cards. There should always be 6 cards in the middle.

7. When you cover a big array, you can collect the "match." While playing, keep a list of the dimensions of the large array and the smaller arrays:

$$7 \times 6 = 3 \times 6 + 4 \times 6$$
$$42 = 18 + 24$$

8. If you run out of cards, take 4 cards from the deck. The game is over when there are no more cards or no more matches can be made.

Factor Cards

2	**2**	**2**	**3**
3	**4**	**4**	**5**
6	**7**	**8**	**9**
12	**15**	**16**	**20**
wild card	**wild card**	**wild card**	**wild card**